The Bubble.io Breakthrough

Build Powerful Web Apps Without a Single Line of Code

By Daniel Melehi

©2025

Contents

The Bubble.io Breakthrough: Build Powerful Web Apps Without a Single Line of Code – Introduction

WHY I WROTE THIS BOOK

I remember the exact moment I realized I wanted to build web applications but had little interest in diving into the complexities of traditional software development. Lines of cryptic code, late nights spent debugging, and the constant cycle of updates felt like an insurmountable barrier. Yet, the drive to create something meaningful—an app that could potentially reach hundreds, thousands, or even millions of users—kept me going. At first, I dabbled in various tools and read scattered blog posts, but nothing seemed to click until I stumbled across Bubble.io. Instantly, I felt the surge of possibility. Here was a platform that promised to let me build my vision without requiring me to master advanced programming languages.

Over the following months, I poured my energy into discovering every detail Bubble had to offer. My journey was both exhilarating and filled with challenges. When I finally launched my first fully functional app—without writing a single line of custom code—I knew that this was a breakthrough worth sharing.

I wrote "The Bubble.io Breakthrough: Build Powerful Web Apps Without a Single Line of Code" for anyone who has ever dreamed of turning an idea into reality but felt intimidated by the complexities of coding. Whether you're an entrepreneur, a creative, or someone simply exploring new career paths, I believe this book will show you the potential of no-code development through first-hand experiences, tips, and best practices.

MY NO-CODE EPIPHANY

The term "no-code" is becoming a buzzword in the tech world, but when I first heard it, I was skeptical. What does "no-code" even mean? Can an application be truly scalable and robust without a single snippet of custom code? I set out on a quest to find out. Bubble.io was the revelation. Not only could I set up a dynamic website, but I could also integrate complex features, design databases, and orchestrate user flows in a way that once seemed reserved for professional software engineers. Yet, I wasn't bending over backward to memorize syntax or debug code. I was working in a visual environment that turned my vision into a tangible product.

That initial spark quickly ignited a passion for exploring this alternative way of creation. Like many, I believed that building a comprehensive web application demanded rigorous study of programming languages. But with Bubble, I discovered that if you can think logically and understand how to piece together building blocks, you can craft a top-tier application. This shift in perspective was incredibly liberating. I want to pass on that sense of freedom to you, dear reader, because I believe there's a creator inside each of us, waiting for the right set of tools to open the floodgates of innovation.

HOW THIS BOOK IS STRUCTURED

Before we dive into the chapters, I'd like to provide a quick overview of how this book is organized. First, I'll walk you through the broader idea of no-code in Chapter 1: The No-Code Revolution. We'll discuss how the tech landscape has evolved, what no-code tools mean for businesses and individuals, and why you should be excited about Bubble.io in particular. Next, in Chapter 2: Setting Up Your Bubble.io Account, I'll guide you step-by-step through account creation, ensuring you're well-prepared to follow along with hands-on exercises.

Chapter 3: Navigating the Bubble Interface focuses on helping you become comfortable with Bubble's design environment. We'll look under the hood of the user interface, exploring each panel, button, and dropdown that you'll need to master. Chapter 4: Key Bubble Concepts lays the foundation for the rest of the journey. We'll define terms like Elements, Workflows, and Data Types so you have a firm grip on how they come together to power any application you wish to build.

EMBRACING CREATIVITY AND VISION

Throughout each chapter, I'll share personal anecdotes and insights to make the learning journey feel like a one-on-one mentorship. I encourage you to approach Bubble.io with an open mind and a willingness to experiment. Don't be afraid to think big. After all, the essence of no-code development is to enable you to innovate without the hurdle of years-long coding training.

Each new feature you build, and every workflow you design, will bring your ideas one step closer to reality. And believe me, there is nothing quite like seeing your vision unfold in a fully functional web application.

So, let's embark on this exciting journey together. By the end, you'll hold in your hands not just a collection of chapters, but a comprehensive roadmap for bringing your concepts to life. I hope you'll find that the best part of this book is the realization that no-code isn't just about side-stepping traditional coding—it's about unlocking your most dynamic, creative potential. Now, let's dive in and explore how Bubble.io can help you forge something remarkable.

Chapter 1: The No-Code Revolution

A NEW DAWN IN DEVELOPMENT

When I first heard people talking about the "no-code revolution," it sounded more like a marketing gimmick than a real movement. But then I remembered how technology had evolved over the decades. Tasks once reserved for experts—like creating a website—had gradually become more accessible thanks to user-friendly platforms. The same principle holds true for application development. In a world where software powers entire industries, why shouldn't the ability to create it be extended beyond those who are fluent in programming languages?

No-code platforms like Bubble.io represent that paradigm shift. They transform development into a visual, highly intuitive environment. Instead of typing commands, you drag and drop elements onto a canvas. With that single change, the logic barrier that once separated programmers from non-programmers starts to dissolve. This shift isn't just about convenience: it's a fundamental rethinking of who gets to invent, innovate, and shape the digital landscape. We're seeing ideas take root that might never have seen the light of day had they required advanced coding skills.

THE DEMOCRATIZATION OF TECH

I've always believed that the best ideas can come from anywhere—artists, writers, accountants, entrepreneurs—and not just from professional developers. No-code tools empower people from these diverse backgrounds to bring their unique insights into the tech sphere. When we lower barriers, creativity flows more freely. You get a broader spectrum of innovations, from simple everyday solutions to large-scale platforms that challenge established market players.

Take, for instance, the small business owner in a rural community who needs a custom application to manage local inventory. Or think about a group of nonprofit volunteers who want to build a digital donation system. These folks might not have the resources to hire a development team, nor the time to learn multiple coding languages. By embracing no-code, they can translate their needs directly into an app without funneling funds into specialized labor. This democratization fosters an inclusive environment where, truly, anyone can be a creator.

SHIFTS IN ECONOMIC AND EMPLOYMENT LANDSCAPES

The no-code revolution is also reshaping professional paths. I've met freelancers who once struggled to find client work because coding projects required them to compete with established agencies. After adopting Bubble.io, they discovered a new niche: building tailored apps for small businesses that never would have considered a custom platform. What used to cost tens of thousands of dollars in development fees can now be done faster and more affordably, opening doors for both developers and their clients.

Consider the corporation that wants to streamline internal workflows. Traditionally, they'd commission a consultant or an in-house dev team to code a solution from scratch. With no-code, even their internal staff can evolve into "citizen developers," experimenting with product ideas and rapidly prototyping new features. This not only saves time and money, but it also instills a culture of innovation where everyone is encouraged to think like a problem-solver.

WHY BUBBLE.IO LEADS THE PACK

With multiple no-code platforms on the market, what makes Bubble.io so special? In my experience, Bubble stands out for its extensive functionality and supportive community. It encompasses all the crucial elements of modern app development, covering design, logic, data, and workflows in one cohesive interface. You're not restricted to a small range of templates or simplistic apps; you can build just about anything your imagination conjures—marketplaces, social networks, dashboards, or even sophisticated SaaS products. Additionally, Bubble's active forum, extensive plugin library, and range of tutorials ensure you'll never feel like you're venturing alone into uncharted territory.

Think of Bubble.io as your launchpad. It isn't merely about skipping lines of code; it's about focusing on the core idea, the user experience, and the real-world value your application delivers. When I realized I could push updates without editing reams of code, I felt liberated to iterate and improve my projects at a pace that would have been impossible using traditional methods. This power to move quickly—to pivot, test, and adjust—captures the essence of the no-code revolution, and it's the reason you're about to embark on a transformative journey.

Chapter 2: Setting Up Your Bubble.io Account

REGISTERING AND GETTING STARTED

I can vividly remember the mix of anticipation and uncertainty when I signed up for my Bubble.io account. It felt like registering for a ride into uncharted territory. However, within minutes, I realized how smooth the process was. To begin, all you need to do is head to Bubble.io's official website. There, you'll see a prompt to create an account using an email address or a social login. I chose to create mine with a dedicated email, but people who prefer the quick route can opt for Google or other social accounts.

Once you fill in the necessary details—name, password, and email—you'll receive a confirmation link. Clicking that link finalizes your registration, and just like that, you gain access to Bubble's core functionalities. It's straightforward, and best of all, you can start building your first app immediately. In my experience, the feeling is akin to stepping onto a never-ending playground, where every corner holds a new way to experiment or solve a problem. If you're anything like me, you'll find it delightfully addictive.

CHOOSING A PLAN THAT FITS YOUR NEEDS

Bubble offers different pricing tiers—from a free plan perfect for experimentation to more advanced ones suited for serious production. Initially, I stuck to the free plan so I could get comfortable with the platform. But as my confidence grew, I saw the value of upgrading. Each plan comes with varying levels of server capacity, collaboration tools, and custom domain options. Think about your project's goals, whether it's a hobby, a proof of concept, or a business venture. That reflection helps in deciding which plan aligns best with your aspirations.

One of the biggest revelations I had was that you can create a fairly sophisticated app on the free plan before encountering any rigid limitations. This lets you experiment at your own pace, refine your concept, and see if your idea really resonates with potential users before you spend any money. By doing that, you transform your development process into a lean, smart, and user-driven endeavor. I can't tell you how satisfying it was to watch my app evolve without feeling financial pressure at every step.

FAMILIARIZING YOURSELF WITH THE DASHBOARD

After logging in, you'll land on the Bubble.io dashboard—a central hub that displays all your projects. Each project is a separate app or environment, and you can create multiple projects to test different ideas. You can even invite collaborators if you're on a plan that supports team development. This dashboard quickly becomes your creative launchpad. A few clicks is all it takes to switch from project to project, checking analytics, adjusting settings, and designing entire user experiences in near real-time.

From this hub, you can rename projects, duplicate them for faster iteration, or delete those you no longer need. It's like having an organized workshop where you can store all your prototypes in marked boxes so you never mix one idea with another. In my case, I set up distinct folders for various projects—an e-commerce concept, a booking application, a social community site—each with a unique name and color-coded icon. This might seem like a small detail, but it's these little organizational habits that can save you a ton of time down the road.

COMMUNITY AND RESOURCES

One of the most helpful aspects I noticed right from day one is Bubble's robust community. The platform is anchored by an engaged forum where you can pose questions, share successes, or learn from others' experiences. When I first started, I turned to these forums quite often—whether it was to figure out how to create a particular workflow or to troubleshoot a database schema. More often than not, a passionate Bubble user or even a member of Bubble's team would jump in with a helpful response.

On top of that, Bubble offers a comprehensive set of tutorials, which guide you through creating simple apps like a to-do list. These tutorials are a fantastic way to grasp the fundamentals of Bubble's interface and logic structures. I still recall the thrill of constructing my first interactive app by following the prompts in a guided lesson. It wasn't just about the end result—it was the sudden confidence boost that came from seeing my ideas work in real-time.

NEXT STEPS

Setting up your account is just the start, but it's an essential milestone in your no-code journey. If you've completed these steps, congratulations—you're officially geared up to translate your dreams into digital experiences. In the next chapter, we'll jump into the layout and navigation of Bubble's interface, breaking down each tool and feature so that you know exactly how to deploy them. You'll quickly learn how to design a user interface, create custom data structures, and set up workflows.

Think of this phase as laying down the foundation for the skyscraper you're about to build. Just as a solid foundation ensures stability, a solid grasp of Bubble's features ensures your future projects will stand the test of scale and complexity. Now that your account is ready, let's move on to exploring the environment that will bring your ideas to life.

Chapter 3: Navigating the Bubble Interface

FIRST IMPRESSIONS

The first time I clicked into the Bubble Editor, I remember being struck by how much functionality was packed into a single screen. Panels on the left and right, a toolbar at the top, and a central workspace beckoning me to drag in elements. It felt like stepping onto the bridge of a spaceship—intimidating, but also thrilling. Over time, I realized that each panel, button, and dropdown has a purpose, and understanding how they work together is like learning the instrument panel of your own creative rocket ship.

The primary sections include the Design tab, where you'll place and edit visual components; the Workflow tab, which controls the logic that makes your app interactive; and the Data tab, where you define your database fields and structure. There are other areas too—Plugins, Settings, and Styles—that offer deeper customization. But for now, I'll focus on the most critical zones so you can hit the ground running.

THE DESIGN TAB

Let's start with the Design tab, which is probably where you'll spend a good chunk of time in the beginning. On the left-hand side, you'll see a palette of elements—text boxes, input fields, buttons, shapes, icons, repeating groups, and more. You can click and drag these onto the blank canvas in the center of your screen. This canvas represents your app's visual layout. If you've ever worked with a graphics editor or a slide presentation tool, you'll find the experience comfortingly familiar.

Yet, there's more than meets the eye. Each element has properties—like width, height, color, style, and dynamic data. When you select an element, the property editor on the right side of the screen changes to let you adjust these attributes. For instance, you might want a button to say "Sign Up," change its background color to green, or make it display a user's name if they're logged in. The design process becomes a playful exploration of possibilities, and because changes appear in real-time, it's instantly rewarding.

WORKFLOWS: THE APP'S BRAIN

Switch over to the Workflow tab, and you'll uncover the logic engine powering your app. Bubble workflows are composed of triggers and actions—when the user clicks a button (trigger), you can create a new record in your database or navigate to a different page (action). Visually, you'll see boxes and arrows that link each step, making conceptual flow easier to understand. Think of workflows as the story arcs that define your app's narrative: user logs in, user sees content, user interacts with the content, and so on.

One of the most remarkable aspects of Bubble is that you configure these workflows entirely through dropdowns and expression builders. There's no code to type, just logical decisions to make. When I grasped that I could orchestrate a complex chain of events—like sending emails, updating records, or recalculating user metrics—without having to memorize syntax, I felt like I'd discovered a creative superpower.

DATABASE AND DATA STRUCTURES

Next, let's turn to the Data tab. Here's where you define your data types—akin to database tables—and the fields that belong to each type. For example, you might create a "User Profile" data type with fields like name, email, and profile picture. Then, whenever someone signs up, Bubble automatically adds a record to this data type for you to reference later. Creating or modifying these structures is straightforward, with point-and-click controls instead of SQL queries or schema files.

Initially, I viewed data as this abstract concept best left to experts. But Bubble's tabular interface demystified it. You can see each record in real-time, filter them, count them, or run searches to fetch specific entries. Understanding your data is key to building apps that are dynamic and responsive to user interactions. Picture it like the backbone of your app—if the data is well-organized, your entire project runs more smoothly.

THE POWER OF REUSABLE ELEMENTS

One feature that frequently comes in handy is the ability to create reusable elements. Let's say you have a header or footer that appears on multiple pages. Instead of adding them manually to each page and constantly updating them, you build them once as a reusable element and drop it where needed. It's similar to using a master slide in presentation software. This approach not only saves time but also maintains a consistent look and feel across your app.

I recall the first time I made a reusable navigation bar. I placed all my main menu links, icons, and a user profile picture in one chunk. Then, whenever I needed a navigation bar on a new page, I just inserted that element. Done. As you grow more comfortable with the interface, you'll discover ways to leverage these reusable elements to keep your app organized and reduce the chance of missing changes in scattered pages.

TIPS FOR EFFICIENT NAVIGATION

As you explore the Bubble Editor more, you'll notice helpful shortcuts. You can group elements to move or style them collectively, or you can right-click to duplicate them. In the property editor, you can define conditional statements—like changing a button's color when the user hovers over it. Keep in mind that each new feature you discover adds a layer of depth to how you design and manage your app. The learning curve might seem steep, but the payoff is enormous once you grasp how each part of the interface works together seamlessly.

Navigating the Bubble interface is much like learning to drive a car. At first, each button and knob can feel a bit overwhelming, but soon it becomes second nature. Once you're comfortable, you'll focus less on how to operate the controls and more on where you want to go creatively. In the next chapter, we'll deepen our understanding of key Bubble concepts so you can design with even more confidence.

Chapter 4: Key Bubble Concepts

ELEMENTS: THE BUILDING BLOCKS

One of the most eye-opening moments in my no-code journey was realizing how crucial each individual component is to the app-building puzzle. In Bubble, these fundamental pieces are called Elements. They range from simple text boxes to complex repeating groups that draw data from the database. If you think of your app as a house, Elements are the bricks. You can stack them in different configurations, apply different finishes, and arrange them into functional rooms.

But they're more than just static visuals. Each Element can display dynamic data from your database. For instance, a text Element might show a user's name once they log in, or a repeating group might generate a list of products pulled from your inventory. Whenever I'm architecting a new page, I start by asking myself: What data do I need to show, and which Elements will best convey that information to users? This question grounds my creative process in actionable steps.

WORKFLOWS: TRIGGERS AND ACTIONS

We touched on workflows in the previous chapter, but let's delve deeper. In Bubble, Workflows represent the logic and user interactions that bring your Elements to life. Think of every button as a potential starting point for a workflow. When a user clicks it, the workflow might do something as simple as show a hidden Element—or it could initiate a multi-step process involving data creation, email notifications, and a page redirect.

One example from my early days was the classic "Sign-Up/Log-In" workflow. When a user clicks the "Sign Up" button, Bubble triggers an action that collects the user's email and password, then saves that information in its built-in User data type. In parallel, you might send a welcome email or update a "User Count" field in your own analytics data type. The key is to think in terms of cause and effect: When this event happens, do these things. This approach transforms your thinking from writing lines of code to orchestrating well-defined steps.

DATA TYPES AND FIELDS

Every dynamic app revolves around data, and in Bubble, data is organized into Data Types. A Data Type is essentially a template or a blueprint for a category of information. Each occupant of that category is called a Thing or a Record. For example, if you have a "Job Posting" Data Type, each individual job listing is a record within that type. Fields serve as the properties that describe these records—such as title, description, salary range, and application deadline.

When you combine Data Types with user actions through workflows, your app starts to feel alive. A new job listing form you build might save all its inputs—position title, location, salary—into the "Job Posting" data type. Then, a repeating group on a different page can fetch and display all the available jobs from that type. By comprehending the relationship between Data Types, Fields, and Workflows, you'll gain a solid grip on how data moves through your application.

CONDITIONS AND STATES

Conditions and States are two concepts that elevate Bubble beyond simple site builders. Conditions let you alter the appearance or behavior of Elements based on specific circumstances. For example, you could change a button's color if a user's input is invalid, or hide an entire group if a user isn't logged in. These conditional rules enhance user experience by making interactions more responsive and intuitive.

States, on the other hand, serve as temporary variables that can store information in a page's memory without writing anything to the database. Let's say you want to remember a user's selection from a list but don't need to save it permanently. You can store that selection in a custom state. This approach keeps your database clean and your interface snappy. I often use states for filtering lists, toggling between different view modes, or managing short-term data that's relevant only for a particular user session.

STYLES AND REUSABILITY

Styles in Bubble act like global CSS templates for your Elements. Setting up a consistent style for buttons, text, and input fields ensures a cohesive look throughout your app. When you change a style, every Element that inherits from it updates automatically. This saves a ton of time, especially when your app grows large. Reusability is a recurring theme: repeated patterns, repeated logic, repeated designs. Bubble's infrastructure supports it at every corner—such as with reusable Elements, repeating groups, and even pre-defined conditions you can copy and paste.

In my own projects, I usually define a brand palette and typography in the Styles tab before I place anything on the canvas. This ensures that all my headings, paragraph text, and buttons share the same aesthetic. It also makes it easier for collaborators, because they can design new pages while staying true to the overall brand identity.

PUTTING IT ALL TOGETHER

When you're first starting out, these concepts might seem like separate puzzle pieces—Elements, Workflows, Data Types, Conditions, and Styles. The magic happens when you see how they interlock to form a complete solution. Let's imagine a simple user registration flow: You have a sign-up page built with text inputs (Elements), a button that triggers a workflow to create a user record in the User data type, a condition checking if the email field is valid, and a style that adjusts the button's hue based on user interactions. Each piece works in tandem, resulting in a process that feels seamless to the end user.

Uncovering how these concepts intertwine is one of the joys of working with Bubble. You'll quickly learn that the possibilities for automation, design flair, and real-time interactions are limited primarily by your imagination. In the chapters ahead, we'll expand on these fundamentals, exploring more advanced features like custom events, integration with external APIs, and tips for scaling. For now, knowing these core ideas is enough to confidently approach just about any app you want to build. Embrace the tools, take them for a test drive, and watch your ideas transform into interactive experiences.

Chapter 5: Designing Your First Page

THE BLANK CANVAS

I vividly recall the first time I gazed upon Bubble's empty design canvas, ready to assemble my very first page. It felt a lot like staring at a blank painter's canvas—so many possibilities, but also a twinge of intimidation. Where do I even begin? One of the most liberating aspects of Bubble's interface is the drag-and-drop freedom. With a few clicks and a dash of creativity, I could place a text field here, a button there, and images exactly where I imagined they'd go. This tactile style of arranging elements reminded me of crafting collages in my school days, but with far more potent tools at my disposal. Each new placement, each tweak in sizing or color, made my page less of an abstract vision and more of a tangible reality.

STRUCTURING YOUR VISION

Designing your first page is truly about translating what's in your head into a coherent layout. Before jumping in, I like to sketch a rough wireframe on paper—just enough structure to guide my design decisions. Then, I start adding elements in Bubble, aligning them visually and making sure everything looks balanced. If you're aiming for a clean, modern feel, you might opt for generous white space and minimalistic fonts. If it's a vibrant landing page, you can experiment with bolder color palettes and playful icons. This planning stage helps ensure that each section of the page—with its headlines, images, or user input forms—

contributes to a purposeful flow rather than a random assortment of items.

ALIGNING AND LAYOUT TOOLS

One of the early lessons I learned was how crucial alignment is to the overall user experience. Even if a single button is located just a hair off-center, it can disrupt the page's aesthetic harmony. Thankfully, Bubble's alignment guides and layout containers are there to keep everything neat. You can group elements, center them, or distribute them evenly—so your page doesn't just look better, it also works better. I also discovered that using layout containers, like columns and rows, can be a powerful way to manage how elements respond at different screen sizes. Rather than manually adjusting for each device, these containers help ensure your design remains consistent, so visitors see a well-organized page whether they're on a phone or a desktop.

INCORPORATING BRANDING AND STYLE

When you're crafting your first page, it's easy to forget the value of consistent branding. I learned the hard way that shifting color schemes on each new section or page confuses users and undercuts your app's credibility. Choose a color palette and stick to it—your page will feel so much more cohesive. I remember picking a muted yet friendly pair of hues for my app's background and buttons, ensuring they complemented each other on every screen. Within the Styles tab, you can define your own heading, subheading, and paragraph formats. This approach streamlines future design work and creates a sense of professionalism. Moreover, do consider accessibility—contrasting colors and legible font sizes go a long way in making your page usable for everyone.

BRINGING IT ALL TOGETHER

After placing your elements, finessing your color schemes, and aligning them just so, the next step is previewing. With a single click on the Preview button, you see how your design comes to life in real time. It's a moment filled with excitement—and a touch of nervousness—because that's when you spot minor misalignments or awkward spacing. Don't be discouraged if the preview doesn't match your vision on the first try; design is an iterative process. Tweak a font size here, adjust a margin there, and re-check. Each update brings you closer to the polished look you're aiming for. Eventually, the page you once envisioned takes actual shape. And in that moment, you realize you've built something that's not just visually pleasing, but also a functional starting point for your users.

Creating your first page in Bubble is more than a simple drag-and-drop exercise—it's your first real taste of weaving visual design and user experience into a single canvas. This is where the magic begins. You've now laid the cornerstone of your future application, setting a visual and functional standard that every subsequent page will match, if not surpass. The process is both exhilarating and a bit humbling, but it also fuels the desire to keep building. Once you hit that final save, you're no longer just imagining an app—you're actively creating something that people can see, touch, and interact with.

Chapter 6: Using Workflows for Dynamic Interactions

SEEING THE BIG PICTURE

I remember the moment it clicked for me: Bubble is more than just placing static elements on a page—it's about breathing life into them. That's where workflows come in. A workflow is essentially a sequence of actions that your app performs in response to a specific event. In other words, whenever a user clicks a button, hovers over a link, or inputs data, you decide what happens next. The first time I set up a workflow to toggle a hidden group was a small revelation. In an instant, my app had gone from a static display to a living, breathing interface, and I felt like I'd unlocked a secret ingredient to user engagement.

TRIGGERING THE MAGIC

Bubble offers a variety of triggers: "When Button is Clicked," "When Input's Value is Changed," "When Page is Loaded," and so forth. Each trigger opens the door to a multitude of actions—creating new data, sending customized emails, showing or hiding an element, navigating to a different page, or even running custom JavaScript with a plugin. Early on, I found it helpful to map out what I wanted each action to accomplish. Take a simple login process: the trigger is the "Login" button click, and the actions might include validating user credentials, updating the user's record, and directing them to the dashboard page if valid. This helps me keep track of the story each workflow tells.

CONDITIONAL LOGIC AND BRANCHING

One of my favorite workflow features is conditional logic. It empowers you to create branches in your app's storyline based on user input or database values. Let's say you have an e-commerce site, and you want to only let users proceed to checkout if they've added at least one product to their cart. You'd set up a condition that checks if "Cart's Item Count > 0." If it is, you move them along; if not, you display a friendly pop-up reminding them to add items first. It's a simple concept, but it adds an invaluable layer of interactivity and personal touch to your app.

CHAINING MULTIPLE ACTIONS

When I first dabbled in workflows, I assumed I'd only run one action per trigger. I was delighted to learn I could chain multiple actions together to form more complex sequences. For instance, upon registration, I might want to create a new user record, send them a welcome email, update a "User Count" statistic, and navigate them to a personalized welcome page—one trigger, four actions, all in sequential order. This chaining makes your app feel cohesive, because a single user action can cascade into multiple features that feel instant and natural. It's the kind of smooth experience people appreciate when they interact with modern web apps.

TESTING AND REFINING

Much like design, workflow building is an iterative process. I learned early on that building a new workflow calls for thorough testing. There were times I clicked my button expectantly, only to watch nothing happen. In those moments, I jumped straight into Debug Mode—a lifesaver within Bubble that lets you step through each action and see where things might be going off track. Maybe I forgot to set a condition properly, or I referenced the wrong data type. Each misstep was a learning moment, sharpening my skill in constructing logical, user-friendly flows. Over time, I realized the hallmark of a strong workflow is clarity in its purpose. If you find yourself adding too many conditions or actions for a single trigger, it's often a nudge to simplify the user journey.

Workflows don't just handle user events; they also handle behind-the-scenes tasks that keep your application running smoothly. You can schedule database cleanups, trigger monthly notifications, or automate data analysis jobs without ever writing complex scripts. It's easy to forget that beneath each polished user interface lies a well-choreographed network of workflows. When done right, the user won't even notice the complexity—everything just works. And that's exactly the feeling you want to evoke, because it gives people confidence in your platform and keeps them coming back for more.

Chapter 7: Database Basics in Bubble.io

MY FIRST DATA ROADMAP

When I first started with Bubble, databases felt like uncharted territory. Words like "tables," "fields," and "queries" conjured images of complicated SQL commands. Fortunately, Bubble's data system spared me from diving deep into code. Instead, I got a highly visual environment that made building my own data structures feel downright approachable. The first app I created needed to store user-generated content and profile information. In traditional coding, that might mean wrestling with server settings and designing a database schema from scratch. But in Bubble, I simply opened the Data tab, created a "Post" data type with fields like "Title," "Content," and "Author," and watched it take shape right before my eyes.

DEFINING DATA TYPES

Each new feature I add to my app usually starts with a question: "Does this require a new data type, or can I extend an existing one?" If I'm tracking a user's activity logs or storing images for a gallery, I might create a data type named "ActivityLog" or "Photo." Each data type becomes a container for various fields—text, number, date, yes/no, or even another data type for creating relationships. The magic of Bubble shines brightest when you realize that you can link data types together. For example, a "Post" data type might reference a "User" data type as its author, making it simple to retrieve user information every time you display a post.

FIELDS AND THEIR IMPORTANCE

Fields are essentially the characteristics of each data record. When I first added a "Title" field to my "Post" data type, I chose "text" as the field type, and all future posts automatically carried that property. By meticulously planning field types, you control the structure of your data. This might not seem vital at first, but it becomes crucial as your app grows. Accidental mismatches—like storing a date in a text field—can complicate your workflows, especially if you need to sort or filter data by date. Being deliberate ensures you can easily query or manipulate data in ways that feel natural. I learned that clarity in naming fields goes a long way, too—something as simple as "postTitle" or "postDate" can save you future headaches.

DATA STORAGE AND PRIVACY

When I made my first interactive app, I realized how important it was to control who could see or modify certain data. Bubble's privacy rules let you define constraints such as "Only allow this user to see these records if they match the user's role." For example, a teacher might see all students' grades, but a student should only see their own. Getting familiar with these privacy settings early on saves you from awkward or even risky revelations of data later. A strong privacy framework ensures that as your user base expands, everyone's information remains protected. It also fosters trust, which is especially critical in apps handling sensitive or personal data.

DISPLAYING AND MODIFYING DATA

One of the most gratifying moments in my Bubble journey was seeing data come alive on the page. Once I had a "Post" data type, I could use repeating groups to pull all the posts from the database and display them in a list—titles, descriptions, authors, and more. Any time I updated a post or added a new one, my page automatically refreshed to show the new data. This real-time interaction isn't limited to text. If you store images or files, Bubble can display them with equal ease. And if you need to edit data from the front-end, it's as simple as creating a workflow that modifies the relevant record. That fluidity dissolved my old fear of databases, replacing it with a sense of creative freedom.

Understanding the basics of Bubble's database tools is your gateway to building dynamic apps that respond to user interactions, produce analytics, and adapt over time. As you layer on more data types and fields, you'll find more advanced techniques—like linking data types together or building complex search constraints. But at the core, it all begins with these process-friendly fundamentals. Once you've seen how intuitive data management can be without a single SQL query in sight, you'll be itching to explore more advanced use cases in your subsequent projects.

Chapter 8: Innovative UI/UX Elements

FROM ORDINARY TO ENGAGING

Early in my Bubble journey, I realized that even the most efficient app can feel dull if its user interface lacks personality. We live in an era where people expect sleek, intuitive experiences, and merely placing fields and buttons on a page can fail to captivate. So, I began experimenting with elements that made each screen feel more alive. One of my first breakthroughs was adding a **hover animation** to buttons, which subtly nudges them upward when users hover over them. It's a small touch, but it adds a layer of interactivity, giving users a gentle cue that the button is clickable. This simple tweak opened my eyes to the power of micro-interactions and how they can elevate the user experience.

MICRO-INTERACTIONS AND FEEDBACK

When we talk about micro-interactions, we're referring to those tiny moments that occur for a singular task—like tapping a like button, receiving a slight vibration, or seeing a heart icon fill up with color. Bubble provides ways to replicate these engaging patterns through conditional statements, animations, and states. An example that stands out is a progress bar I once created for a survey app. After each question, the bar would smoothly transition to indicate progress. It was more than just a visual flourish; it gave users a sense of accomplishment as they advanced. By focusing on these details, your app feels less like a static page and more like a responsive companion guiding users along their journey.

POPUPS AND MODULAR WINDOWS

Popups can be a game-changer for user experience, especially when you want to display focused information or gather input without redirecting users to another page. I used to think popups were strictly for alerts or warnings, but Bubble's flexibility allowed me to turn them into mini-workspaces. I created a payment form that appeared in a popup, letting users settle transactions in one streamlined step. Additionally, for user onboarding, I designed popups that gave short tips and tooltips while the rest of the screen dimmed. Each popup can contain its own elements and workflows, granting a self-contained environment to accomplish specific tasks quickly.

CUSTOM ANIMATIONS AND TRANSITIONS

In my quest to make each feature stand out, I started dabbling in Bubble's transitional effects—fade in, slide out, or even create your own sequences if you're feeling ambitious. For instance, let's say you have a sidebar that stores a user's settings. Rather than having it visible all the time, you can keep it hidden and trigger a slide-in animation when the user clicks a settings icon. It feels polished and reduces visual clutter. Carefully chosen animations can guide user attention to priority actions or messages. However, I've also learned that overdoing it can be distracting. The trick is to employ transitions that serve a function—enhancing clarity or delight—without overwhelming the core interaction.

PERSONALIZATION AND RESPONSIVE LAYOUTS

A friend once told me, "An app that acknowledges me by name instantly feels more welcoming." Bubble excels at personalizing user interfaces because its data connection allows you to pull user-specific information into nearly any element. Displaying someone's name, profile photo, or custom recommendations on the homepage cultivates a sense of belonging, prompting users to engage more deeply. This concept extends to responsive design, too. With Bubble's responsive engine, you can ensure that the polished, interactive interface you've crafted adjusts gracefully on various screen sizes. A layout that looks great on a desktop might need a different arrangement on mobile—Bubble's responsive settings let you define how elements realign or resize without needing external CSS frameworks.

Innovating your UI/UX isn't about tossing in flashy elements at random; it's about crafting a cohesive experience that resonates with your user's goals and emotional journey. Each small enhancement, from color schemes to animation and personalization, weaves into the overall tapestry that is your brand's story. By thoughtfully incorporating engaging elements and intuitive navigation paths, you create an environment where users feel both guided and inspired. After all, a memorable experience goes beyond functionality—it's the sense of possibility and delight that encourages people to come back, share your app, and grow into loyal advocates.

Chapter 9: Integrating APIs Seamlessly

STEPPING BEYOND YOUR APP'S WALLS

Not long after I got comfortable with Bubble's native features, I encountered a challenge: I needed my app to fetch real-time stock prices and incorporate them into a dashboard. It quickly dawned on me that Bubble alone couldn't generate that data—so I had to reach outside my app's "walls" using an API. An API, or Application Programming Interface, is a doorway to external services, letting your app both send and receive data and commands. At first, I was apprehensive because dealing with APIs sounded like hardcore programming. But Bubble's API Connector plugin changed that perception. Suddenly, I could link to external data sources and seamlessly integrate them into my workflows. It was like discovering a hidden superpower for my app.

SETTING UP THE API CONNECTOR

Bubble's API Connector plugin is your starting point for weaving external services into the fabric of your application. Once installed, you'll find a dedicated area where you can define API calls—think of them as recipes for requesting or sending data. For example, if you're using a weather service, you'd specify endpoints like "Get current weather data," define any parameters (location, units, etc.), and configure how Bubble should parse the returned JSON. To a newcomer, these steps might look technical, but Bubble guides you through them by providing fields for URL, method type (GET, POST, PUT), and headers for authentication tokens. Completing one or two examples is usually enough to grasp the fundamentals.

AUTHENTICATION AND SECURITY

One aspect that initially tripped me up was authentication—verifying that my app had the right to access someone else's data. Many APIs use methods like API keys, OAuth 2.0, or JWT tokens to ensure data remains secure. I had to carefully read the documentation for each service I connected to, figuring out if I needed to pass a token in the header or request a spinning token from an authorization server. While it's not as simple as plugging in a phone charger, it's also far less complicated than writing raw code. Once you configure your authentication steps in Bubble, your valid credentials are stored securely, so you don't have to re-enter them every time you make a call.

DISPLAYING AND MANIPULATING EXTERNAL DATA

After setting up the API call, the real fun begins—presenting the fetched data to your users. Let's say you're displaying live tweets about a certain hashtag. You could store them in a custom data type or simply show them in a repeating group. I remember the first time I built a currency converter app. I used an API to fetch the latest exchange rates, stored them briefly in the database, and even let users search historical data for better context. This integration gave my app a sense of sophistication; it no longer felt like a closed loop. But it's important to remember that external data can change unpredictably, so you'll want to handle errors and limit data calls to avoid performance hits.

WORKFLOWS WITH EXTERNAL ENDPOINTS

The potential for workflows expands dramatically once you incorporate APIs. For instance, you can establish a workflow that triggers at a specific time each day to pull updated prices, user analytics, or weather forecasts—automatically refreshing parts of your application without user involvement. You can also push data out to other platforms. Imagine a scenario where each sale in your Bubble app pings a fulfillment API that manages shipping labels, then sends a notification email through a separate mailing service. This interconnected approach transforms Bubble into a command center, orchestrating tasks across multiple platforms with minimal friction.

Embracing APIs can feel like you've burst into a much larger world, where your single Bubble app is just one star in a vast galaxy of services. For me, it was an eye-opening moment that illustrated how powerful no-code could really be. Rather than coding from scratch, I was connecting puzzle pieces—each representing a specialized function offered by some online service. The result was an app that felt more robust, dynamic, and up-to-date than anything I could have built in isolation. By mastering this skill, you future-proof your application, ensuring it can grow and adapt as new possibilities arise in our ever-evolving tech landscape.

Chapter 10: Visual Programming Best Practices

EMBRACING A VISUAL MINDSET

When I first dove into Bubble's visual programming approach, I noticed it required a shift in mindset. Traditional programming coerces you to think in terms of syntax and logic flow, while visual programming nudges you to conceptualize features as building blocks that fit together. One of the earliest tips I discovered was to picture your entire application as a living diagram. Buttons, text fields, workflows, and database connections all work together, forming a sort of map. By imagining how these components link, you can anticipate potential issues ahead of time. For me, it felt akin to painting a mural; each brushstroke is purposeful, but you need to see the entire canvas to ensure consistency.

One best practice I adopted was spending a few minutes sketching ideas before opening the Bubble editor. I jotted down the pages I needed and the broad strokes of how they'd interact— login screens, dashboards, pop-ups, data inputs. This quick exercise minimized guesswork when I started dragging and dropping elements. If something didn't match my plan, that was an immediate cue to refine my overall layout so that the visual logic never felt haphazard.

LOGICAL LAYOUTS AND GROUPING

A piece of advice I often share is to lean on grouping techniques. When you group elements, you not only keep your editor tidy but also ensure your workflows remain intuitive. Let's say you're designing a settings page with numerous toggles and user preferences. Grouping each set of toggles under a labeled container helps you quickly see where to attach relevant workflows. It also keeps your interface from turning into a scattered mess. Over time, you'll discover that grouping eliminates extra steps when you need to move or hide multiple elements simultaneously.

Moreover, naming each group thoughtfully is worth the extra few seconds. Generic labels like "Group A" or "Group 1" can cause confusion down the road. Instead, if you use "Group – User Settings" or "Group – Email Preferences," it's instantly clear what's inside the container. This clarity pays off when your app grows in complexity, or when you're collaborating with others who might not be as familiar with your initial design decisions.

LAYERING CONDITIONS AND STATES WISELY

Bubble allows you to apply multiple conditions to a single element. While this flexibility is empowering, it can also lead to cluttered or contradictory states if you're not careful. I found it helpful to prioritize which condition should take precedence. For example, if you have a button that turns red when no input is provided and green when the input meets certain criteria, you don't want a secondary condition overriding that color without reason.

A tidy workaround is to rely on "When Condition is True" statements with well-defined logic. Consider labeling them: "No Input = Red," "Valid Input = Green." This approach ensures you don't accidentally step on your own toes by piling too many conditional statements. Also, paying attention to Bubble's condition order and whether those conditions are mutually exclusive can save you from head-scratching moments later, when your button unexpectedly flips back to a previous color.

COMMENTING AND DOCUMENTATION

When I first ventured into Bubble, I underestimated how quickly a project's logic could become complex. Between hidden elements, workflows, and data connections, it's surprisingly easy to lose track of how one tweak might affect another. That's why I started documenting each major workflow using Bubble's built-in note fields and comments. After creating a workflow, I'd add a short explanation: "Sends verification email on user sign-up" or "Filters the list by date before displaying it."

At first, it felt like a chore, but it proved invaluable whenever I returned to a project months later. It's also a boon for teamwork: if someone else steps into your project, they'll be able to navigate the logic with minimal confusion. Plus, these annotations make debugging far less daunting. If an issue arises, I can read through my notes and see exactly what I intended each workflow to do, which speeds up the troubleshooting process significantly.

ITERATING WITH CLEAR VERSION CONTROL

Visual programming thrives on iteration. You'll frequently adjust layouts, refine workflows, or incorporate new data structures. One lesson I learned is to always take advantage of Bubble's versioning system. Each time I reach a meaningful milestone— like adding a new user role or integrating a complicated data call—I'll create a new version of the app. That way, if something goes awry, I have a fallback point that I can easily roll back to.

I've also adopted a naming convention for these versions: "v1.0 – Basic Layout," "v1.1 – Added Search Feature," and so on. This habit keeps me organized, especially when juggling multiple improvements at once. And if a user reports that a bug appeared after a certain feature launch, I can pinpoint which version might contain the glitch. It's a safeguard that makes experimentation less risky.

Overall, visual programming best practices stem from a commitment to organization, clarity, and forward-thinking. By structuring your app logically, labeling every piece of your puzzle, layering conditions judiciously, documenting workflows, and harnessing version control, you'll ensure your Bubble project remains approachable even as it grows. For me, adopting these habits transformed my workflow from casual tinkering into a disciplined creative process, enabling me to build more powerful and efficient apps without introducing the chaos that often accompanies rapid development.

Chapter 11: Deploying Your MVP

FROM PROTOTYPE TO PUBLIC

When I embarked on my first Bubble project, I remember the day I decided it was ready for a broader audience. My excitement blended with trepidation, as I worried about everything from performance to user feedback. But I knew that if I waited for "perfect," my app might never see the light of day. That's when I became determined to embrace the Minimum Viable Product (MVP) mindset. An MVP is your opportunity to share a workable version of your idea, gather insight, and refine it using real-world data, rather than assumptions.

During those early phases, Bubble's platform was a godsend. Because no-code allows for rapid iteration, creating a functional MVP took weeks instead of months. Even so, I quickly learned that deploying an MVP isn't just a matter of clicking "Publish." It involves strategic planning—and a bit of mental fortitude.

POLISHING THE ESSENTIALS

Before pushing your MVP out, it's wise to revisit your user flows. Are they intuitive enough that a new user can sign up, navigate the core features, and achieve their main objective without confusion? I remember user-testing my first app with a few friends and family members. Even though I was certain it was clear, they stumbled over steps that seemed obvious to me. That feedback led me to simplify onboarding logic, add clearer error messages, and reduce redundant fields on sign-up forms.

By focusing on the essentials, you're delivering value as soon as possible. Real-world feedback is infinitely more valuable than speculation, so keep your MVP feature set tight. Avoid the temptation to load up on every interesting feature you can imagine. Users might get overwhelmed, or even worse, find your app confusing. Less can often be more, especially in the early stages.

PREPARING FOR LAUNCH

Once I narrowed down my MVP's scope, I turned to Bubble's deployment tools. On the free plan, you can run your app in a test environment indefinitely. But when it's time to go public, you'll either map a custom domain to your project or use Bubble's default subdomain. Mapping a custom domain can establish credibility—people often trust an app that looks like a legitimate website. Configuring a domain through your registrar is straightforward, as Bubble provides clear instructions on DNS settings.

Another step that many first-time publishers overlook is setting up SSL certificates for secure browsing. Bubble automatically offers free SSL for apps on custom domains, which reassured me that users wouldn't see those scary "Not Secure" warnings in their browsers. Handling user data responsibly is crucial, so robust security measures are a must from day one.

SCALING AND PERFORMANCE CONSIDERATIONS

After deployment, I watched anxiously as users began to sign up and share feedback. One surprise was how quickly performance issues could arise when multiple people were repeatedly testing the same flows. Although Bubble handles server scaling behind the scenes, there are ways to keep your MVP running efficiently—like minimizing large image files, optimizing repeating group queries, and limiting unnecessary workflows.

I also learned the importance of logging and monitoring. Bubble's logs let you see if any errors pop up, and you can check CPU usage to ensure your app isn't overloading. These metrics might seem unimportant in the early stages, but they help you identify bottlenecks. Because the MVP is a stepping stone to a fully-fledged product, it's best to iron out performance kinks sooner rather than later.

GATHERING FEEDBACK AND ITERATING

The biggest payoff of releasing an MVP is the data you collect: user behavior, sign-up drop-off points, and direct feedback on what they love—or don't love—about your app. After each new wave of insights, I would jump back into Bubble to refine the design or add requested features. This feedback loop felt like a dance: I'd build, they'd react, I'd adjust, and so forth. Over time, the app evolved into something more polished and user-friendly than I could have designed on my own.

At times, I ran A/B tests—giving one group of users a page design and another group a slightly different layout. Bubble's quick deployment cycles allowed me to track which variant performed better, then commit to the winning design. This data-driven approach made me more confident in my decisions, because I wasn't guessing—I was listening.

Ultimately, deploying your MVP is both a milestone and the start of a deeper relationship with your user community. By focusing on polished core features, ensuring secure and stable performance, and remaining open to user-driven improvements, you turn your MVP into a living laboratory where ideas flourish and transform into tangible results. For me, that initial launch step felt exhilarating, reminding me that the real adventure begins when your app meets the very people it's meant to serve.

Chapter 12: Handling User Authentication

THE GATEWAY TO YOUR APP

If you're anything like me, the word "authentication" used to conjure images of cryptic code libraries and complex security protocols. When I built my first application in Bubble, I was pleasantly surprised at how straightforward user authentication can be. Bubble provides out-of-the-box account creation, password handling, and login/logout workflows—all without requiring you to write a single line of code or juggle multiple security packages. This convenience allows you to dedicate more mental energy to crafting an excellent user experience and less on wrestling with authentication complexities.

SIGN-UP FLOWS AND CUSTOM FIELDS

The first step to building a comfortable authentication experience typically involves designing a sign-up flow. For my projects, I begin by asking myself: What user information do I truly need at this stage? Required data might be as simple as an email and password, but you can also collect details like username, profile image, or role (e.g., admin, vendor, customer). In Bubble, these fields seamlessly align with the built-in User data type, and adding custom fields is as easy as naming them: "Role," "Address," "SubscriptionStatus," and so on.

By integrating only the essentials up front, you reduce friction for new users. You can always create an expandable profile page later, giving them the option to add more details when they're ready. This approach not only streamlines the sign-up process but also reduces the chance of overwhelming newcomers with too many questions.

SECURING PASSWORDS AND SESSIONS

One of the biggest worries I had was about password security—nobody wants to be that person who causes a data breach. Thankfully, Bubble manages password encryption and session handling in the background. Each user's password is hashed, so your database never stores it in plain text. Moreover, session tokens are handled automatically, reducing the chance of unauthorized access.

I make it a habit to encourage strong passwords by adding a simple password strength checker or providing guidelines above the password field. Although it's optional, it fosters good security practices and reassures users that you're safeguarding their data. Bubble's built-in email verification option is also straightforward to configure; just enable "Require email confirmation" in your app settings, and Bubble will send out verification links.

FORGOT PASSWORD AND ACCOUNT RECOVERY

I've locked myself out of enough accounts to realize how critical a user recovery path is. Bubble includes a "Forgot Password" workflow that allows you to email a reset link to the user. It's plug-and-play. You can jazz it up by customizing the email's design or adding a personalized message.

If you need more advanced recovery options—like security questions or a multiple-step verification—you can build those flows with Bubble's workflow engine. Whenever I create such features, I keep user empathy in mind. People are often frustrated when they've forgotten their password, so a clear, concise recovery process can turn their annoyance into relief.

SOCIAL LOGINS AND OAUTH

Enabling social logins—like Google or Facebook—can streamline the registration process by letting users log in without memorizing another username and password. Bubble's plugin library provides pre-built integrations for popular social networks. Once installed, you configure the plugin with the required keys (provided by the social platform), and you instantly have a "Login with Google" or "Login with Facebook" button.

Be sure to verify the data that flows back from these providers. For instance, you might want to store the user's Google profile image or Facebook name in your User data type. This convenience can do wonders for your onboarding rate, as it reduces friction for new sign-ups.

LAYERING ON ACCESS CONTROLS

After you've handled basic sign-ups and log-ins, you can set more nuanced permissions. For a membership site, you may have "premium" users with exclusive page access or "admin" users who can moderate content. Bubble's privacy rules let you define who can view or modify data based on user roles. Whenever I'm building an app that includes an admin dashboard, I ensure that the relevant data types are visible only to admins. This approach is not only secure but also helps maintain a clean interface, preventing non-admin users from stumbling onto pages or data they shouldn't see.

It's a thrill to see users truly engage with your application— posting, commenting, or making purchases—knowing that their information is locked behind robust authentication protocols.

My biggest takeaway is that user authentication is not a dreaded chore when working with Bubble; rather, it's an opportunity to design a welcoming and secure experience. By leveraging built-in tools for sign-up flows, password security, recovery options, and role-based access, you can take a huge leap forward in user trust. After all, trust is the foundation upon which every successful app is built, and this foundation starts the moment a user creates an account.

Chapter 13: Scheduling Custom Events

SEIZING THE POWER OF AUTOMATION

I remember the day I decided my app needed an automated nudge: I wanted to send out gentle reminders to users who hadn't completed their profile within a certain timeframe. Before Bubble, my mental model of scheduling tasks involved cron jobs, third-party schedulers, and complicated scripts. Yet in Bubble, orchestrating behind-the-scenes activities often requires nothing more than a few clicks in the workflow interface. Scheduling custom events became my secret weapon for operating essential processes without any ongoing manual intervention.

UNDERSTANDING SCHEDULED WORKFLOWS VS. RECURRING WORKFLOWS

In Bubble, two key approaches exist for time-based automation: Scheduled Workflows and Recurring Workflows. Scheduled workflows let you program a one-time or repetitive action for a future point in time—like sending a reminder email after seven days. Recurring workflows, on the other hand, can operate at a fixed cadence, such as running every hour or every week. I quickly realized recurring workflows were perfect for housekeeping tasks, like removing expired records or archiving old data.

Identifying which method aligns with your goal is crucial. If you want a workflow to run once after a certain event, scheduling it is straightforward. If your task calls for indefinite repetition, turn to recurring workflows, but mind your app's performance and plan usage, since you might be running these tasks often.

BUILDING TIME-BASED TRIGGERS

Designing a custom event in Bubble starts by defining the workflow you want to run. For example, let's say I want to check if a user finished filling out their account details one week after sign-up. I create a workflow called "Send Profile Completion Reminder" that sends an email to the user. Next, whenever a new user registers, I schedule that workflow to fire exactly seven days later, with the unique user data supplied as parameters. Bubble handles the rest behind the scenes.

I enjoy how intuitive it feels to link user-specific data into the scheduled event. If the user updates their profile before the seven-day mark, I can cancel or adjust that scheduled task, preventing redundant notifications. This interplay of conditionals and scheduling fosters a personalized experience—no wasted emails to users who've already completed the necessary steps.

AUTOMATING COMPLEX PROCESSES

At one point, I built an e-commerce application requiring routine price checks. Each day at midnight, the system would ping an external API to retrieve updated product costs, then recalculate any relevant discounts. This entire chain of events happened while I slept—and it felt magical to see updated pricing automatically appear in the morning. Scheduled events made my app feel alive.

In more advanced scenarios, you can sequence multiple custom events for sophisticated operations. For instance, you might schedule a data cleanup event, followed by an event that sends summary reports to admins. By breaking complex tasks into smaller, scheduled components, everything remains neatly organized within your Bubble application itself, reducing the need for external integrations.

MONITORING AND TROUBLESHOOTING

Once your custom events are live, it's a good practice to monitor their activity. Bubble's "Logs" section shows you whether the scheduled workflows succeeded, failed, or even triggered at the appointed time. If something doesn't look right—like an email never arriving—you can review the log to pinpoint the issue. Maybe you used an incorrect parameter or an expired API key. Either way, the information is there to guide your debugging process.

I also discovered that building test custom events in a development version of my app is a best practice. That way, if you inadvertently schedule an event that loops too often or hits performance bottlenecks, the potential impact is limited. Once you're confident in the results, you can push it to the live environment.

Implementing scheduled custom events takes your Bubble app to the next level. No longer do you need to rely on user prompts or manual triggers. You can keep your application fresh, timely, and responsive—even when no one is actively on the site. For me, discovering this feature drove home how truly advanced no-code development can be. Being able to automate vital processes in a matter of minutes is nothing short of liberating, giving you and your users more time to focus on what really matters: accomplishing meaningful tasks within your application's ecosystem.

Chapter 14: Working with Plugins

EXPANDING BEYOND THE STANDARD TOOLKIT

Not long after I gained confidence in Bubble's built-in features, I found myself wanting more specialized capabilities—like advanced data visualization or custom chat widgets. That's when I ventured into the plugin ecosystem. Plugins are pre-built modules that add functionality beyond the standard Bubble toolkit. They range from simple UI elements to intricate integrations, and they enable you to deploy new features rapidly without coding them from scratch. Think of them as power-ups in a video game: each install grants you new abilities, saving the time and hassle of reinventing the wheel.

EXPLORING THE PLUGIN MARKETPLACE

Bubble's plugin marketplace is where you'll likely start. The sheer variety can be both exhilarating and overwhelming, especially if you're not sure what you're looking for. I recall feeling like a kid in a candy store—spreadsheets, chart libraries, login integrations, payment gateways, and more. My advice: approach the marketplace with a clear objective. If you need real-time messaging, type "chat" in the search bar and compare the available plugins. Evaluate their ratings, documentation, and any support forums to be sure they're actively maintained.

I once underestimated this vetting process and installed a plugin that hadn't been updated in a while. It slowed down my app with subpar code and created compatibility headaches. So, read user reviews or reach out to the developer if you have questions. A well-maintained plugin can be a game-changer, while a neglected one might become a liability.

INSTALLING AND CONFIGURING PLUGINS

Installing plugins is straightforward. In the Plugin tab, search for the one you need and click "Install." Once it's in your project, you'll see a settings page where you can input any required credentials or parameters—like API keys for a payment gateway.

After that, the plugin typically appears among your design elements or workflow actions. For instance, if it's a charting plugin, you'll be able to drag-and-drop a chart element onto your page and link it to your data.

Configuration is where novices sometimes trip up. Each plugin has a unique set of instructions, so pay attention to the documentation. If the plugin calls for certain data fields or a specific workflow sequence, replicate exactly what's outlined. Also, don't be shy about testing thoroughly. I usually create a "plugin playground" page in my Bubble project to experiment with the new element, ensuring it behaves as expected before integrating it into my main interface.

CUSTOMIZING PLUGIN BEHAVIOR

One of the joys of Bubble is the freedom to blend plugin functionality with your own logic. Let's say you've installed a video player plugin. You can set a dynamic URL field so that different pages load different videos, or add workflow events that trigger actions once a video ends. If the plugin supports custom states or offers additional styling, you can incorporate them to maintain the look and feel of your brand.

I remember a project where I combined a chart plugin with scheduled workflows. Each morning, the app fetched new data from an external API, updated the database, and automatically refreshed the chart. This harmony between Bubble's built-in features and the plugin's specialized capabilities gave my app a polished "wow" factor I would have struggled to achieve on my own.

BUILDING OR COMMISSIONING YOUR OWN PLUGIN

At some point, you may find no existing plugin fits your needs perfectly. That's when you face a fork in the road: craft a custom plugin yourself or commission someone else to do it. If you have a bit of JavaScript knowledge, Bubble's plugin builder interface isn't as intimidating as I initially imagined. You can define plugin elements, states, and actions, bridging them into Bubble's environment. It's an excellent chance to combine minimal coding with no-code convenience.

Alternatively, you can hire someone from Bubble's developer community or external marketplaces. I once commissioned a custom plugin for a specialized scheduling system. While it cost me time and money, it paid off by perfectly solving a challenge that off-the-shelf plugins couldn't address. Plus, owning a custom plugin means you can update it as your app's demands evolve.

In the end, working with plugins in Bubble is all about striking a balance between what's available off the shelf and what you might need to build. By taking the time to vet plugins, install them properly, and integrate them thoughtfully into your workflow, you can enrich your Bubble app with minimal fuss. The possibilities are staggering: interactive maps, machine learning add-ons, gamification elements, you name it. Through this expansive plugin ecosystem, Bubble continues to break the boundaries of no-code, proving that even advanced, feature-rich apps are well within reach for makers of all backgrounds.

Chapter 15: Scaling in the Cloud

THE EVOLUTION FROM SMALL TO BIG

I still remember the excitement of releasing my very first Bubble app to a handful of friends and watching them log in for the first time. That initial user base was small enough for me to tackle any performance hiccups manually. But as months passed, I began to see sign-ups climb steadily, and the cracks started to show. My once-simple workflows were working overtime, and the server logs hinted at growing stress. That was when I realized I needed to prepare my Bubble application for a bigger audience—one that could come knocking all at once.

Fortunately, one of the benefits of Bubble is that it's built on a robust cloud infrastructure. It's designed to accommodate everything from small prototypes to fully operational platforms with thousands of users. But "built-to-scale" doesn't mean you can ignore best practices. It's still crucial to understand how cloud-based resources expand, contract, and handle the unpredictable traffic patterns that come with online growth.

UNDERSTANDING BUBBLE'S AUTO-SCALING

In my early days with Bubble, I assumed that the platform would magically handle every surge without me lifting a finger. While Bubble does take care of a lot—like distributing server loads and managing updates—there's more to the picture. Bubble offers auto-scaling on higher-tier plans, allowing your application to tap into extra server capacity when user loads peak. This approach means that if you hit an unexpected rush of traffic, your app won't necessarily slow to a crawl. However, as you scale up, you'll notice the cost structure also changes to mirror that capacity.

I learned to stay mindful of usage metrics. The logs and analytics Bubble provides can be your best friend. For instance, if you detect that workflows are taking too long during peak hours, consider either streamlining those workflows or upgrading your plan. By proactively monitoring usage, you avoid the dramatic scenario where users can't load pages because of resource constraints.

DESIGNING FOR HORIZONTAL GROWTH

One of the biggest mistakes I made in my early attempts at scaling was assuming that I could just pump more capacity into my app. Scaling effectively also requires you to think about how the app is structured. The concept of "horizontal growth" comes into play here—distributing the workload across multiple areas. For example, you might offload heavy computations to background workflows or shift large file handling to specialized services.

I remember building a data visualization feature that crunched a massive dataset in real time. Everything worked fine when I tested it alone, but as more users accessed it simultaneously, it bogged down the entire site. My eventual solution was to move that computation into a scheduled workflow that ran every 30 minutes, caching the results for quick display. This extra layer improved the user experience and prevented my app from stalling under load.

LEVERAGING EXTERNAL SERVICES

As your Bubble app grows, you might find special cases where you need an extra boost. For instance, you might need an external database for advanced querying or a dedicated search service for lightning-fast lookups. At one point, I added a feature that required an AI algorithm to classify images. Instead of attempting to replicate that within Bubble's environment, I connected to a specialized AI service via APIs. This small decision offloaded a resource-intensive task, allowing Bubble to focus on managing front-end interactions and user workflows.

I also started using CDNs for images and static files. This approach not only sped up delivery times but scattered the load across multiple servers worldwide. Users in different regions could access resources from the closest node, reducing latency. Incorporating such external services may initially feel like a big step, but it can do wonders for both speed and reliability once your user base gains global traction.

PLANNING FOR THE UNEXPECTED

One lesson my mentor impressed upon me—"Always plan for success." That might sound obvious, but how many of us truly prepare for the day thousands of people flood our site overnight? I certainly didn't at first, and it led to frantic late-night scrambling when a viral post suddenly tripled my traffic. Since then, I've added load testing to my workflow. Tools and scripts can simulate big groups of users hitting the same page or function. By measuring how well my Bubble app copes, I can detect performance bottlenecks before real users encounter them.

It's not just about system strain, either. Budget constraints can be a limiting factor. A surge in usage might require a higher plan or more external resources, so keep financial projections in mind. Scaling in the cloud is about balancing costs with capacity. I've learned to treat my scaling strategy as a living blueprint: I periodically reexamine it, adjusting capacity, removing unused plugins, and optimizing workflows.

In the end, scaling in the cloud with Bubble isn't about flipping a single switch for infinite growth. It's a thoughtful process of tuning your application architecture, watching performance metrics, preparing for sudden waves of interest, and knowing when to tap into external services. This balancing act ensures that as your user base multiplies and your mission expands, your app is ready to rise to the occasion—rather than buckle under the weight of its own success.

Chapter 16: Building Complex Data Structures

RETHINKING DATA BEYOND BASICS

When I started working in Bubble, creating data types felt like a breeze. It was easy enough to store user profiles, blog posts, or basic product listings. As my projects matured, however, I ran into the need for data structures that better mirrored real-world relationships. An app for real estate, for instance, might have data types like "Property," "Agent," "Buyer," and "Appointment." Each had to reference the others in ways that allowed for robust filtering and workflow logic. That meant going beyond a single, flat data type and instead orchestrating a network of interlinked records.

Bubble's no-code approach made it less scary to experiment. I started seeing my database not as a series of tables, but as a living tapestry of data points—each referencing and communicating with the other. It wasn't long before I was tackling advanced relationships such as many-to-many or even polymorphic links where one field could adapt to differently typed data.

MAPPING OUT ENTITY RELATIONSHIPS

I vividly recall a complex scenario: building a delivery platform where drivers could have multiple routes, each route could pass through multiple drop-off points, and each point could be linked to specific customers. Sketching those relationships on paper was my lifesaver. I identified each major entity (Driver, Route, Drop-Off Point, and Customer) and how they connected. In Bubble's editor, I created data types for each entity, then used fields like "List of Routes" on the Driver data type and "List of Drop-Off Points" on the Route.

This hierarchical mapping ensured that I could quickly access relevant information. For instance, if I needed to view a driver's entire day, I'd simply reference that driver's "List of Routes," and for each route, I could pull up the "List of Drop-Off Points." The key challenge was keeping it clean and intuitive—too many nested lists can become a maze.

WORKING WITH JOINED TABLES AND LINKING FIELDS

Admittedly, Bubble doesn't use the conventional SQL schema. The relationships are more dynamic, as you can directly store references to entire data objects or lists. I learned that, in many cases, you can replicate joined-table functionality by adding a "linked" field to one or more data types. For example, a "Project" data type might have a field called "Team Members," which is essentially a list of Users. Meanwhile, each User could have a field called "Projects_involved_in," which is a list of Projects.

This flexibility makes it remarkably simple to query data. If I need to find all team members for a project, I look at the project's "Team Members" field. If I need to find all projects a user is part of, I do the reverse. I love how intuitively this mirrors real-world logic—"What tasks are you assigned?" becomes "What tasks are in your record?" But I also learned to be cautious in how many linked fields I create. Over-complicating references can make data retrieval slow and housekeeping tricky if records change or require deletion.

NESTED REPEATING GROUPS AND DATA DISPLAY

One of the joys of mastering complex data structures is seeing them spring to life on your pages through nested repeating groups. Let's say you're building an educational platform. You might display a repeating group of "Courses," and inside each course, another repeating group of "Modules." The modules could include a repeating group of "Lessons," and so on. This nested arrangement can look quite elaborate, yet Bubble's interface handles it gracefully.

However, my experience has taught me to keep an eye on display speed. If each nested repeating group tries to load hundreds of records, your users might be staring at an empty screen for a while. Consider pagination, or load data incrementally. That way, you preserve a quick, responsive feel while still showing the depth of your data relationships.

VERSIONING YOUR DATABASE SCHEMA

Complex data structures often need iterative refinement. In the early days, I felt anxious each time I changed a field name or added a new data type, fearful of breaking existing features. Eventually, I embraced Bubble's versioning system. This approach lets me test schema adjustments in a development environment before pushing them live. If something doesn't work, I revert with minimal fuss.

I also learned to keep a cheat sheet: "In version v2.1, switched 'Customer' field from single item to list." Having these notes helps me track my schema evolution. If an issue pops up, I can locate exactly when I made the database change that likely triggered it.

MAINTAINING DATA INTEGRITY

The deeper your relational web grows, the more vital it becomes to maintain data hygiene. I realized I needed workflows or early validations to ensure, for instance, I didn't remove a user record that other parts of the database still reference. Understanding how Bubble's "cascade delete" or "unlinking" might work in these scenarios is critical to prevent orphaned records. Sometimes, I'd build an "on delete" workflow that checks if a particular record is still in use, displaying a warning if references exist. While slightly more work, these checks safeguard against the heartbreak of broken links and missing data.

Mastering complex data structures in Bubble is like learning a new language of relationships. At first, it might feel daunting, but once you see how each piece can fit snugly together—users, products, reservations, pick your scenario—it starts to make perfect sense. The platform's visual database tools are a huge advantage, letting you mold data in fluid ways without writing formal SQL or maintaining complex migration scripts. And that, in my view, is the sort of autonomy that keeps creativity at the forefront of no-code innovation.

Chapter 17: Performance Optimization

UNEARTHING HIDDEN BOTTLENECKS

The first time my Bubble app slowed to a crawl, I was blindsided. I'd designed a slick interface, integrated essential workflows, and tested it with a small focus group—everything seemed fine. Then, as my user base grew, screens would freeze halfway through loading, and I'd get frustrated messages about how "the site was taking forever." So began my adventure into performance optimization. It turned out that a few unsuspecting workflows and large data queries were strangling my application's speed.

Performance optimization in Bubble often comes down to examining each layer: database queries, on-page calculations, and data display elements. Resolving problems meant stepping back, uncovering those inefficiencies, and trimming them one by one. Each improvement brought a tangible sense of relief—faster page loads, happier users, and a steadier experience overall.

STREAMLINING WORKFLOWS

One major culprit I found was overly complex workflows. Early on, I had a sign-up escape room game that involved five or six actions triggered simultaneously by a single button. While fun conceptually, it bogged down everything behind the scenes. My solution was to break it up into simpler chains—one action updated the database, another triggered an email, and a custom event handled data checks in the background.

Instead of locking up the user interface while everything processed, I spread the load out so the UI remained responsive. If a workflow felt like it needed more advanced logic, I often used scheduled workflows to handle large tasks off the main thread. This tactic turned out to be a game-changer because it prevented user-facing delays and allowed me to focus on a smooth, frictionless experience.

OPTIMIZING DATABASE QUERIES

When it comes to data retrieval, a heavier search query can easily clog performance. Early in my Bubble career, I set up complicated nested searches—some referencing fields in multiple related data types. It worked brilliantly for me during private tests with minimal data. But once real-world users started dumping thousands of records, each search took a noticeable toll.

I began using advanced filters and constraints to narrow down the dataset before loading it onto the page. This approach proved vital: Bubble can quickly handle smaller sets of records, but huge lists can sap speed. If I needed to display large volumes of information, I learned to paginate—loading a portion of the data at a time. This method gives users immediate access to the first batch, while the rest quietly loads as needed.

LEVERAGING CACHING AND REUSABLE ELEMENTS

Another technique that saved me was caching frequently used data. If I had a list of categories or a set of user settings required across multiple pages, I'd store them in a custom state or a small data type. The next time the user navigated, Bubble wouldn't need to re-fetch the same data from the database. Sure, it meant I had to manage how often I updated that cache, but the trade-off for speed often justified the extra steps.

Reusable elements also eased the load. By creating a shared navigation bar or form component, I ensured Bubble didn't have to rebuild these elements from scratch every time. This approach might appear minor, but it accumulates noticeable performance gains as your app grows in complexity.

MANAGING VISUAL ASSETS

Images, videos, and other heavy media can choke your site's loading speed just as effectively as a dense query. I learned to compress images before uploading them to Bubble, and I considered third-party hosting for particularly large files. If you want a hero image on your landing page, that's great—but an uncompressed, high-resolution file might balloon your load times. Tools like TinyPNG let me shrink image sizes without significant quality loss, and that change alone snagged me several seconds of improvement on lower-bandwidth connections.

CONTINUOUS MONITORING

Performance isn't a one-and-done affair; it's an ongoing effort. After making adjustments, I often monitored my logs in Bubble to see if error rates dipped or if certain workflows no longer spiked in runtime. Spreading out usage tests is also wise. Some of my clients were in different time zones, so a surge of traffic might come while I was asleep. Having an automated alert system that flagged unusual response times saved me from nasty surprises in the morning.

Occasionally, I'd run my application through tools like Google PageSpeed Insights—though keep in mind, those are tailored primarily to traditional websites. Still, it can point out glaring issues, such as unoptimized images or excessive scripting. The key is to keep an eye on real-user behavior. If people start measurably dropping off, that's a clue your site isn't performing up to snuff.

By continually refining workflow logic, optimizing data queries, efficiently handling visual assets, and adopting a rigorous monitoring routine, my Bubble apps evolved into much smoother experiences. The best validation, of course, came from user feedback. Fewer complaints about sluggishness and more comments about convenience signaled that I'd finally turned the corner on performance woes. And let me tell you, nothing beats the rush of seeing a feature-heavy Bubble app perform swiftly and gracefully—an achievement that felt almost magical in a no-code world.

Chapter 18: Testing and Debugging

WHY TESTING BECOMES YOUR BEST FRIEND

I used to dread testing. Early on, I'd wrap up a feature, eyeball it for obvious mistakes, and launch. But after a few user complaints about broken buttons or missing data, I realized just how vital a thorough testing phase can be. Testing isn't about fault-finding for the sake of negativity; it's a proactive measure to ensure the final user sees a well-oiled application. In Bubble, you're shielded from the nitty-gritty of coding bugs, but that makes functional and user experience (UX) testing all the more essential. Even well-constructed workflows or data structures can yield unexpected results if they're not tested systematically.

I began to see testing as a creative challenge. Rather than something I did grudgingly at the end of a project, I integrated it into my daily production cycle. Each time I introduced new data types or complicated workflows, I carved out a small chunk of time to poke, prod, and attempt to break them. The goal was to spot issues before my app reached unsuspecting users.

USING BUBBLE'S DEBUGGER

Bubble has a built-in debugger that can walk you through each workflow action step by step. I can't count the number of times this tool has saved me. Let's say you're testing a sign-up process: in debug mode, you can see if "Step 1: Create account" fires off successfully or if an error occurs. Then you track whether "Step 2: Send welcome email" triggers properly. It's like shining a flashlight into the inner workings of your app, revealing logic flows that might otherwise remain hidden.

You can also simulate different speeds (slow, normal, fast) to watch transitions happen in quasi-real time. This perspective can help isolate issues where elements load out of sequence, especially in data-heavy pages. If something fails, the debugger typically logs a message describing the failure's cause ("Email not sent—invalid email address" or "Data field not found"). That clarity guided me through more than one dicey fix, especially when juggling multiple custom states or nested references.

SETTING UP A DEDICATED TESTING ENVIRONMENT

When I first learned about Bubble's development and live environments, I found it tempting to test everything right in "Live." After all, it worked for small changes, right? But the moment I tried more drastic modifications—a new payment module, major UI rearrangements—it became obvious that testing in development was the only safe path. In the development environment, you can break things, push them to their limits, and revert changes without panicking about live users refreshing in the middle of your experiment.

These distinct environments also help you maintain separate databases. You can mock up dummy user accounts, fill them with sample data, and run stress tests without corrupting real user data. This division gave me the peace of mind to explore new ideas without jeopardizing my entire platform.

MANUAL VS. AUTOMATED TESTING

One day, after repeatedly clicking through sign-up flows, checking pop-ups, and verifying emails, my wrist felt sore. I realized I needed a more systematic way to test. While Bubble doesn't offer an out-of-the-box automated test suite like some coding frameworks do, you can integrate external services to simulate user interactions. There are tools that can fill forms, click buttons, and take screenshots of each state.

I still believe manual testing is valuable—it provides a user's perspective and can catch aesthetic or logical quirks automated scripts might overlook. But for tasks like creating 50 dummy orders or simulating a group chat with multiple participants, automation can save hours and keep your sanity intact. The key is striking a balance: let automated tests handle repetitive tasks, and use manual checks for user-interface nuances and bespoke workflows.

TROUBLESHOOTING COMMON PITFALLS

Over time, I identified a few recurring trouble spots that demanded special vigilance. Anything related to log-in and sign-up is prime real estate for bugs. A single overlooked condition can block users from accessing vital pages. Payment integrations deserve special scrutiny, too. I once forgot to switch from "Test Mode" to "Live Mode" in Stripe, causing real transactions to fail spectacularly. Another area that demands attention is performance under load. Even if your local tests pass, you need to confirm your app doesn't slow down or stall when multiple people perform the same action.

Whenever I discover a bug, I jot down a short post-mortem note outlining what happened, why, and how I fixed it. This small habit has grown into a personal library of lessons learned, preventing me from repeating mistakes across future projects.

RELEASE WITH CONFIDENCE

The final piece of a strong testing regimen is a well-thought-out release process. Before going live, I run through a final mental checklist: Have I tested all critical workflows? Did I confirm that newly added features integrate smoothly with the old ones? Do I have a rollback plan in case something unexpected surfaces?

Released features don't always perform flawlessly, and I've occasionally had to hotfix small errors. But these fixes are far less disruptive when I've already ironed out the big stuff through rigorous testing. Watching users interact with a new feature—without encountering glaring bugs—makes every hour spent in the debugging trenches worthwhile. It's a moment of pure satisfaction and validation, reminding me that careful testing is as integral to app creation as the bright ideas that spark it.

Chapter 19: Responsive Design Techniques

WHY RESPONSIVENESS MATTERS

I'll never forget checking my app on a friend's phone for the first time, only to discover that the layout looked completely skewed. Images bled off the screen, text boxes overlapped, and certain buttons were completely unreachable. That was my wake-up call: in an era where mobile browsing often surpasses desktop usage, ignoring responsiveness is a recipe for user frustration. Bubble's responsive engine offers a visual way to handle this, but it's not a one-click fix. Properly harnessing its power takes some deliberate thought and experimentation.

The beauty of Bubble is that once you do master responsiveness, your designs can elegantly realign for screens of any size. This means you're not forced to maintain separate desktop and mobile versions, unless your project specifically benefits from it. Instead, you craft one interface that intelligently refactors itself depending on the user's viewport.

BUILDING WITH FLUID LAYOUTS

One of the first techniques I adopted was embracing fluid layouts. Rather than fix the width of a group or repeating group, I allowed them to expand or contract based on the parent container. This strategy ensures content can "breathe" on larger screens without squishing on smaller ones. In practice, it often means setting maximum and minimum widths, so elements don't become comically wide on desktop or impossibly narrow on mobile.

I found that using Bubble's "Align to parent" and "Fixed width" checkboxes carefully can yield a world of difference. If I wanted a navigation bar that stayed consistent across devices, I'd rely on a fixed header, but let its child elements scale proportionally. This approach stopped my logo from ballooning or my menu buttons from clipping out of frame.

GROUPS WITHIN GROUPS

One trick that saved me a ton of frustration was nesting groups. Each group acts like its own container, giving me control over how its child elements adapt to different screens. During one project—a job listing platform—I created a "parent group" to hold the job summary and used nested groups for the title, company logo, and quick apply button. On a wide screen, everything laid out horizontally. On a narrow screen, the logo and title stacked neatly, with the apply button floating below.

Yes, it adds an extra layer of structure to your page, but these group nests can be your best allies when wrestling with unpredictable layouts. The key is to give each group meaningful alignment rules and test them at various breakpoints.

CUSTOM BREAKPOINTS AND CONDITIONAL FORMATTING

While Bubble's default breakpoints cover general ranges, I realized I sometimes wanted more fine-grained control. For instance, in one of my e-commerce apps, I had a promotional banner that looked great on tablets in landscape orientation but tripped over itself in portrait. Custom breakpoints allowed me to hide that banner or swap it for a slimmer version when the width dipped below a certain threshold.

Bubble also lets you apply conditional formatting based on a container's width or the overall page width. I used this technique to swap out large images for smaller, optimized ones on phones, saving both space and load time. By combining custom breakpoints with conditionals, I shaped an interface that truly adapted to each device, rather than shoehorning everything into one layout.

KEEPING TEXT READABLE

Text is surprisingly tricky to manage across devices. A font size that feels perfect on a desktop may be microscopic on a phone. I learned to let text elements scale, by setting relative font sizes or leveraging conditionals. For instance, "When page width < 400, set heading font size to 18" ensures that my headlines remain legible on smaller screens.

I also pay attention to line breaks. Paragraphs that flow nicely on a laptop can suddenly become mile-long columns on a large monitor. Setting an upper limit on column widths preserves readability, so you don't end up with lines that stretch from one side of the screen to the other.

TESTING ON REAL DEVICES AND EMULATORS

After implementing responsive tweaks, the only real way to confirm everything works is hands-on testing. Bubble's responsive preview is a valuable tool, but it's also beneficial to test on actual phones, tablets, and various screen resolutions. I'd borrow friends' devices or use online emulators that replicate multiple screen sizes. Each test helped me uncover minor misalignments I might have missed.

One thing I took to heart: your interface might look polished in Bubble's built-in preview but behave unexpectedly on a real phone. Scrolling behavior, pinching to zoom, or the presence of on-screen keyboards can shift elements in ways you didn't anticipate.

ITERATING FOR A POLISHED FINAL LOOK

Responsive design is never a one-and-done affair. Every time I added a new feature, I had to revisit my layout, confirm everything still felt balanced, and ensure that no element was clipping or overlapping on smaller breakpoints. Over time, I got quicker at anticipating potential pitfalls. If you approach your layout with responsiveness in mind from the start, you'll face fewer headaches than if you retrofit it at the eleventh hour.

In the end, mastering responsive design in Bubble grants you the freedom to engage users wherever they are—on a pocket-sized phone, a mid-range tablet, or a sprawling desktop monitor. By fluidly adapting your layouts and media, you deliver a professional vibe that resonates with modern audiences. And that first time you see your site snap perfectly from landscape to portrait orientation, it's a moment of genuine triumph, proving that no-code doesn't mean no polish.

Chapter 20: Launching Your Application

THE FINAL COUNTDOWN

There's a special kind of thrill that comes with sensing your app is nearly ready to face the outside world. I recall the flutter in my stomach during my first official launch—an exhilarating mix of excitement and nerves. My biggest lesson? The final weeks or days leading up to your go-live date can be a whirlwind of checks, tweaks, and adjustments. By this point, you've likely tested your workflows, polished your visuals, and refined your data structures. Now, it's about trust—trusting the work you've put in, trusting those subtle user feedback sessions, and trusting yourself enough to release your dream to actual, real users.

DOMAIN SETUP AND BRAND CONSISTENCY

One of my first steps before flipping the proverbial "on" switch is to finalize the domain. If you plan to use a custom domain rather than Bubble's default subdomain, mapping it in the settings becomes an important to-do item. I remember wrestling with DNS settings and wondering if I'd accidentally route traffic to oblivion. However, after carefully following Bubble's guides and verifying with my domain provider, the transition was smooth. A custom domain makes your app feel professional—it says, "We're open for business, and we're here to stay."

Branding consistency also extends to details like your app's favicon or social sharing images. These tiny touches might seem optional, but they help shape the first impressions of your audience. For me, making sure I had a recognizable logo and color palette across the landing page, sign-up forms, and email footers underscored a sense of polish. The goal is to show users you've given them a cohesive environment, not a hodgepodge of disconnected screens.

FINAL PRE-LAUNCH TESTING

While you've probably vetted your app's core functionality multiple times, a focused, end-to-end check can reveal last-minute snags. I often enlist a small group of trusted testers—people who will crack open every corner of the app and attempt to break it. This is the moment to confirm that your sign-up flows transition smoothly into onboarding, that your data displays accurately, and that your complex workflows (like payments or file uploads) won't crumble under pressure.

I've found it beneficial to create a "soft launch" environment. Instead of announcing publicly, I quietly release the app to a limited audience, maybe close friends or a small group of beta testers. Their experiences, questions, and bug reports come in fast and unfiltered. This approach spares you from potential public embarrassment and helps ensure the version you present to your wider user base is as stable as possible.

CRAFTING A LAUNCH PLAN

A spontaneous launch might work for personal projects or niche experiments, but if you're aiming for impact, it pays to have a strategy. I like to map out a two-week or one-month plan that includes social media teasers, email newsletters, and maybe a short blog post highlighting the app's unique features. If your platform caters to a specific community—enthusiasts of gourmet cooking, for example—try engaging that group where they already hang out: specialized forums, Facebook groups, or relevant online gatherings.

While hype can be a powerful motivator, overpromising is a pitfall. I've learned to highlight core benefits instead of half-baked features. Users trust you more when you understate your app's abilities and then overdeliver, rather than setting sky-high expectations and failing to meet them.

POST-LAUNCH REFLECTIONS

The actual launch day can feel anticlimactic—sometimes everything goes fine, and sometimes you encounter a flurry of small issues. Either way, this is only the beginning. Observing metrics like user sign-ups, retention, and how people navigate your interface gives you powerful insight for your next steps. I keep a close eye on logs and analytics to diagnose unexpected errors, track usage, and see if certain pages are drawing more attention than others.

If users hit roadblocks, respond quickly. A timely bug fix or a helpful note in your documentation can earn you significant goodwill. After my first major launch, I spent the following week sending personalized emails to early adopters, thanking them and including a quick survey. This direct communication helped me prioritize enhancements for the next update.

Launching a Bubble application is less about fireworks and more about consistency, adaptability, and listening—and that's a great thing. Once you open those virtual doors, real feedback flows in, guiding you toward meaningful improvements. So, yes, enjoy the moment when your project becomes "real" in the eyes of the public. Celebrate your milestone, but keep a pen and paper handy, ready to jot down the bright ideas and lessons that inevitably emerge in those heady first weeks.

And remember: it may be the end of development's intense phase, but it's also the start of an even more interactive—and rewarding—chapter in your no-code journey.

Chapter 21: Monetizing Your Platform

SHIFTING TO A BUSINESS MINDSET

I'll admit, when I built my very first Bubble app, I was more focused on creativity and less on revenue. But after sinking hours into design, data organization, and user testing, I started asking myself: "How do I keep this venture sustainable?" Monetization isn't just about stuffing ads into every corner; it's about structuring your app so that people see value, are willing to pay for it, and feel satisfied that they got their money's worth.

Transitioning from a purely creative or experimental project to a revenue-generating platform often requires a mental shift. You're not just an app builder anymore—you're a business owner. You have to consider your operating costs, your target audience's purchasing behavior, and your growth trajectory. With Bubble's visual interface making the building blocks easier, you can invest more time thinking strategically about pricing tiers, payment methods, and long-term viability.

CHOOSING A MONETIZATION MODEL

Every app is different, so it's worth exploring several revenue streams. Some entrepreneurs opt for a subscription-based model, where users pay monthly or annually for continued access to features. Others offer a one-time purchase or a freemium version, hoping to eventually convert free users into paying customers with premium perks. I once ran a marketplace where I took a small transaction fee from each sale instead of charging membership fees. It attracted people who might otherwise shy away from a recurring commitment.

One approach I've grown fond of is tiered pricing. Users on the "Basic" tier could utilize essential features, while "Premium" or "Pro" subscribers gained access to advanced functionality—like unlimited usage, advanced analytics, or specialized support. Structuring these tiers properly can be a fun puzzle: you want to protect your premium features without stripping the free version of its usefulness.

PAYMENT GATEWAYS AND PLANS

Implementing payments in Bubble isn't daunting—plugins for Stripe, PayPal, and other gateways make the process smooth. After installing the relevant plugin, you can configure it to handle one-time fees, recurring subscriptions, or both. The real hurdle is ensuring you adhere to sales tax or VAT rules if you extend internationally. When I first launched a subscription service, I had to do my homework on tax obligations in different regions. This might not be the most glamorous task, but ignoring it can lead to complications down the road.

Additionally, think about how you'll handle refunds or disputes. Having a clear refund policy can keep you out of messy exchanges. If you're using Stripe, for instance, you can automate parts of the refund process within Bubble's workflows. It's also wise to set up triggers for email notifications, so you're never caught off-guard by a sudden chargeback or payment failure.

IN-APP PURCHASES AND PAYWALLS

For content-heavy apps—like digital magazines, video platforms, or e-learning products—in-app purchases and paywalls might be your route to profitability. Let's say you have a library of premium tutorials. You can segment your database to differentiate free and paid content. Non-paying visitors get a teaser, maybe the first few lessons, while paying members enjoy full access.

Bubble's conditional logic helps here. For instance, you can show or hide entire sections depending on whether a user's subscription status equals "premium." If a user tries to access restricted content, pop up a friendly prompt to upgrade. The key is balancing friction with motivation. You want potential customers to get a taste of what's behind the paywall, yet still make subscribing look enticing.

MAINTAINING USER TRUST

One of the hidden layers of monetization is trust. If you're asking for people's money, they need to feel secure. That often means investing in SSL (which Bubble conveniently provides) and ensuring your privacy policies and terms of service are clear. People respect transparency. Describing in plain language how your billing cycles work—how to cancel, what data you collect—goes a long way in preventing chargeback drama.

Building trust extends to making your app truly valuable. When I arranged personalized coaching features for my platform, I made sure to highlight success stories and user testimonials. If your users believe you're genuinely helping them solve a problem or reach a goal, they're far more likely to pay you consistently.

ITERATING AND GROWING REVENUE

At the end of the day, monetization is an ongoing journey. I regularly experiment with minor price adjustments, promotional discounts, or bundling certain features. I keep an eye on metrics like churn rate and lifetime value—if something spikes or dips unexpectedly, I test a new concept. It's fascinating how a small tweak, like offering a discounted annual subscription, can significantly impact your monthly revenue.

In short, monetizing a Bubble-built platform is about more than bolting on a checkout form. It's a careful dance of understanding user psychology, delivering on tangible value, and managing logistical details like payment gateways and customer support. Once you see those first paid sign-ups rolling in, you realize you've built something that can grow into a sustainable endeavor—one where your passion for no-code development intersects profit, possibility, and lasting impact.

Chapter 22: Designing for Accessibility

A NEW PERSPECTIVE ON INCLUSIVITY

When I ventured into app-building, I was eager to create sleek user interfaces that would dazzle. But as I began sharing my projects more widely, I encountered people who struggled with color contrast issues, complicated navigation, or small text sizes that strained their eyes. Realizing that some individuals couldn't fully engage with my platform due to these design oversights hit me hard. That's when I started exploring the necessity of accessibility in digital experiences—recognizing that an inclusive app isn't just a kind gesture, it's a fundamental requirement for many users.

In Bubble, we're fortunate to have an interface that streamlines many design tasks, but we're still the ultimate deciders of how inclusive our pages and elements become. Over time, I learned that good accessibility practices also often lead to better overall usability—everyone benefits, not just those with specific needs, when an app is straightforward and welcoming.

COLOR CONTRAST AND READABILITY

One of the most overlooked elements of accessible design is color contrast. If your text color and background color are too similar in tone, people with low vision—or even those simply struggling with bright sunlight on their screens—might have trouble reading. I recall an early iteration of my site that used pastel text on a white backdrop because it looked modern. Unfortunately, it was barely legible for many.

Adjusting your palette to meet WCAG (Web Content Accessibility Guidelines) contrast ratios can be a game-changer. Bubble's style settings let you easily modify text and background shades. I use online contrast checkers to ensure my chosen colors pass the recommended thresholds. A small tweak in brightness or saturation can make a significant difference for readability without sacrificing visual appeal.

STRUCTURED NAVIGATION AND HEADINGS

When I discovered how screen readers rely on heading tags to guide users through content, I began paying closer attention to how I structured my layouts. Properly labeling sections with **h1**,

h2, or **h3** headings isn't just about visual hierarchy; it's about enabling assistive technologies to parse content logically.

In Bubble, I frame each main content area with an appropriate heading, then break subtopics into subheadings. If I was building an FAQ page, each question might be an **h2** while each answer kicked off with **h3**. Think of it as a table of contents for someone who can't see the page layout. This approach also naturally improves SEO, which is an added perk.

KEYBOARD-ONLY INTERACTIONS

A factor we often take for granted is mouse-based navigation. Yet some users either prefer or require keyboard navigation. Have you tried tabbing through your Bubble app to see if everything is accessible that way? It was eye-opening for me. I realized certain elements had no focus state, meaning when I tabbed through the page, I couldn't tell which button or link was active.

In response, I started styling focus outlines for buttons and form fields. This way, each element clearly highlights when selected. Bubble supports these styling adjustments in the "Conditions" tab or through custom CSS in the plugin area. Even a simple box-shadow or color change can keep keyboard-only users oriented as they navigate.

ALTERNATIVE TEXT AND DESCRIPTIONS

Visual media often enhances the experience for sighted users but can be challenging for those relying on screen readers. One fix is to add alt text to images—short descriptive tags that convey the image's content or purpose. In my early days, I overlooked alt text entirely, leaving my users in the dark about key visuals. Now, whenever I add an image in Bubble, I fill in the alt text field, ensuring that everyone can follow along.

The same principle applies to video or audio clips. Providing captions or transcripts can help hearing-impaired users or those who can't have audio on at the moment. Designing for multiple senses and scenarios is both considerate and strategic—it extends your app's reach and fosters loyalty among diverse groups.

CONTINUOUS IMPROVEMENT

You don't need to flip your entire design philosophy overnight to become accessible. Small, steady changes can accumulate into a highly inclusive environment. I keep a running checklist of accessibility concerns—things like verifying my color contrast with each design update, ensuring keyboard focus states remain visible, and labeling new interactive elements. Once you cultivate this awareness, it becomes second nature.

It also pays to gather feedback from actual users with varying needs. If you can, invite them to test your app. Their insights might reveal hidden pitfalls or simple opportunities to be more inclusive. Accessibility shouldn't be an afterthought or a novelty—it's a crucial part of building an experience where everyone feels welcomed and valued.

Ultimately, by embedding accessibility practices into your Bubble projects, you're not only meeting ethical obligations but also unlocking a broader audience. Each improvement helps your platform stand out as a considerate, user-focused space. In the process, you'll find your own perspective evolving—designing for accessibility stops feeling like a chore and starts feeling like a natural extension of good user experience.

Chapter 23: Building Community Features

FROM USERS TO COMMUNITY MEMBERS

I began seeing the magic of community-driven apps when I added a simple discussion forum to one of my projects. Suddenly, users weren't just passively consuming information; they were helping each other, offering feedback, and forging genuine connections. That sense of belonging, I realized, is a powerful force. People are far more likely to stick around if they feel they're part of something bigger, a space where their voice has value.

In Bubble, constructing community features is easier than you might think. With dynamic data sorting, user roles, and real-time interactions, you can piece together anything from basic comment sections to full-fledged social networks. Before you dive in, though, it's beneficial to consider how you want your community to function, behave, and evolve.

DISCUSSION BOARDS AND THREADS

One of the most straightforward community features to implement is a forum. Create a data type for "ForumPost," with fields like title, body, author, and timestamps. Then design a repeating group to display them, sorted by the most recent activity. I remember feeling a rush when I watched new posts appear in real time, as if I had my own mini social platform.

You can enhance your forum by nesting "Replies" under each post, effectively creating threaded discussions. Users appreciate organization, so letting them see who replied to whom helps keep the conversation cohesive. Additionally, consider adding features like likes, upvotes, or a "mark as best answer" option if you want to boost engagement. These small interactions can make the community feel vibrant and rewarding.

GROUPS AND SUB-COMMUNITIES

Not everyone will want to participate in the same big conversation. That's why I often segment communities into groups or categories—niche corners where people can discuss specialized topics. In Bubble, you can create a "Group" data type and tie it to your users, so each group has a roster of members.

Maybe you're running an educational platform. You could build a "Courses" section where each course has its own forum or channel. That way, advanced learners can talk in one dedicated space while beginners find comfort in a less intimidating environment. The key is to ensure your navigation makes it easy to find and jump between these sub-communities without confusion.

ENCOURAGING POSITIVE INTERACTION

A community can be a double-edged sword. On one hand, genuine user-generated content is priceless. On the other, there's the risk of trolls, spammers, or heated arguments. Early on, I instituted a simple code of conduct and pinned it at the top of every discussion board. It spelled out the do's and don'ts, like respectful language and zero tolerance for harassment.

You should also consider moderation tools. For instance, you might designate certain users as "Moderators" who can delete inappropriate posts or suspend accounts. Bubble's role-based permissions make this simple to set up. If someone abuses the community, having a clear moderation workflow helps you respond quickly. This fosters a sense of safety and civility.

REAL-TIME CHAT AND DIRECT MESSAGES

Sometimes, a direct chat can bring users closer together than a public forum. Implementing a real-time messaging system might sound advanced, but with the right plugin or scheduled workflows, you can approximate live conversations. I once built a direct messaging feature that updated every few seconds, and the sense of immediacy impressed users.

If you don't have the bandwidth for real-time updates, asynchronous messaging is perfectly fine—users send each other messages, and a notification appears in their inbox. The important part is providing a private channel for them to connect and collaborate in a more personal way.

COMMUNITY GROWTH AND EVENTS

A thriving community often goes beyond text-based discussions. Think about hosting webinars, virtual meetups, or exclusive insider sessions. I've even seen platforms integrate calendars where members can RSVP to upcoming events. Another idea is to award badges or achievements for engagement milestones— like "Top Contributor" or "Helpful Mentor."

User engagement is often linked to how recognized and valued people feel. A small gesture, like highlighting active members, can translate into big loyalty boosts. On the flip side, don't overdo the gamification if your audience prefers a more professional or formal environment. Understand your community's culture and tailor your features accordingly.

Ultimately, building community features in Bubble is about weaving together dynamic data, user roles, and interactive elements so people feel inclined to stick around and interact with each other. The payoff? The more they engage, the more your platform transforms from a mere tool into a living ecosystem— one that can survive and thrive beyond your individual efforts. Whether you're creating a bustling social space or a close-knit forum, focusing on user well-being and positive interactions turns your audience into an enthusiastic community—one that grows and evolves right alongside your core app.

Chapter 24: Email Automations

STAYING IN TOUCH WITHOUT MANUAL EFFORT

Email automations became my best friend after spending weeks doing tasks manually—like reminding users to complete their profiles or following up on abandoned carts. The moment I set up my first automated email sequence, it felt downright magical. I no longer had to babysit a mailing list or individually type messages. Instead, Bubble's workflow logic and third-party email services took care of the heavy lifting, leaving me free to focus on improving other aspects of my app.

Automation isn't about sending endless spam. It's about providing timely, relevant communication. Whether it's welcoming new sign-ups with a mini tutorial or congratulating a user on hitting a specific milestone, thoughtful emails can create a more intimate relationship between your platform and its community.

CHOOSING THE RIGHT EMAIL SERVICE

Bubble gives you the option to integrate with a variety of email services—SendGrid, Mailchimp, Postmark, and more. For transactional emails (like password resets or purchase receipts), I often use SendGrid because its plugin configuration is straightforward, and it offers reliable deliverability. For marketing campaigns or newsletters, services like Mailchimp can provide analytics, subscriber segmentation, and visually appealing templates.

Before connecting anything, check your service's free tier limits, personalization features, and capacity for future growth. Having tens of thousands of users might necessitate a more robust plan—nothing is worse than having a crucial email bounce because you've exceeded your daily quota.

DESIGNING YOUR WORKFLOW

The secret sauce in Bubble-based email automations lies in how you weave workflows with user data. For instance, if you've built an onboarding sequence, you could schedule an email to fire two days after someone registers—providing them with a short checklist of features to explore. Then, on day five, you could send a testimonial or tip from another user, encouraging deeper engagement.

I like to keep a separate "Email Automations" page or section within my Bubble editor where I manage all these workflows in one place. It simplifies debugging and ensures I don't lose track of where messages originate. You can even create custom events—that is, user-defined triggers—like "User hits 10 completed tasks" or "Subscription about to expire," which then fire off a prewritten email.

PERSONALIZING FOR IMPACT

I recall a dramatic improvement when I started inserting user-specific details into emails: a name, a relevant link, or even the data they'd previously entered. Bubble makes this a breeze with dynamic fields. Nothing feels more impersonal than a generic "Hello, user!" greeting. By tailoring the subject line and body text to reflect something about the individual, you're far more likely to catch their attention and keep them engaged.

For instance, if your platform is about fitness tracking, the email could read: "Hey, Sarah! We noticed you crushed your step goal today—awesome work!" That small nod of recognition can incentivize Sarah to open future emails, confident that they're personalized to her journey.

AVOIDING SPAM TRAPS

We've all experienced the agony of legitimate emails ending up in the spam folder. It's crucial to set up proper Sender Policy Framework (SPF) and DomainKeys Identified Mail (DKIM) records for your domain. These DNS-level validations assure email providers that your messages are legitimate and come from who they claim to come from. Most email services offer guided steps to implement these measures.

Additionally, keep an eye on your bounce rate or unsubscribe rate. If too many addresses bounce or recipients mark your emails as spam, mailbox providers might lower your sender reputation, making deliverability even harder. Offer a clear unsubscribe process to avoid forcing your emails onto people who no longer want them—persisting can tarnish your reputation and hamper your entire campaign's reach.

ANALYZING AND REFINING

Automation isn't a set-it-and-forget-it affair. After a couple of weeks or months, analyze your open rates, click-through rates, and conversion data. Are people actually doing what you hope they'll do after reading your emails? If not, tweak your subject lines or rework your calls to action. The data might show that users prefer shorter messages, or that they respond more to a certain style—casual vs. professional, for instance.

One approach I rely on is A/B testing. Let's say you send out two variants of an onboarding email—one focusing on feature highlights, the other telling a success story. Whichever one garners higher engagement becomes your default, and you can test another variation next time. Over repeated cycles, your automated emails become fine-tuned ambassadors for your app.

In the end, email automations serve as a persistent but friendly tap on the shoulder, reminding users that your platform stands ready to help them achieve their goals. By weaving them into Bubble's dynamic data and workflow logic, you craft messages that truly land—both in inboxes and in your users' hearts. That's the magic of letting well-planned sequences handle the heavy lifting while you continue innovating in other corners of your no-code domain.

Chapter 25: Real-Time Updates with Bubble.io

THE THRILL OF IMMEDIATE FEEDBACK

I still remember the electricity I felt the first time my Bubble app updated content before my eyes, without even refreshing the page. It was like stepping into the future—no more hitting F5 or waiting for stale data to vanish. Real-time updates transform your application into a living, breathing platform where users see changes as they happen. This immediacy not only heightens engagement but also deepens trust. Users realize they're not dealing with static pages; they're part of an active, responsive community or workflow.

In my early attempts, I didn't fully grasp how Bubble's infrastructure handled real-time data. Yet once I started exploring the platform's built-in capabilities—things like auto-binding, database triggers, and custom events—I recognized that building a real-time experience was more straightforward than I'd imagined. It wasn't about exotic coding or obscure protocols; it was about leveraging Bubble's logic in clever ways.

HARNESSING AUTO-BINDING AND DATA TRIGGERS

One of Bubble's simplest real-time features is auto-binding, which allows inputs and text fields to sync directly with a database record in near-instant fashion. Rather than manually saving a change, I could let Bubble update the record the moment a user edits a field. That quickness feels almost magical. It's a small start, but it showcases how "instant" your interface can become.

Beyond auto-binding, running database triggers on changes can push updates to other users. I've built social feeds where a new post appears for anyone currently viewing the page, no refresh required. Of course, you need to structure queries in a way that refreshes the correct data sets—particularly if your app deals with high-volumes of content. But once you've nailed that setup, the sense of immediacy can be addicting.

BUILDING COLLABORATIVE EXPERIENCES

A prime example of real-time synergy is a shared workspace or collaborative document. Even though Bubble doesn't natively replicate ultra-rapid Google Docs editing, you can approximate real-time collaboration through frequent auto-refreshing or custom events that pull the latest text from the database. For instance, I once created a brainstorming board where team members could toss in sticky notes simultaneously. A short refresh interval on a repeating group meant everyone saw new notes pop up in close to real time.

If you want more advanced interactions—like seeing another person's cursor position or highlighting text on the fly—you might consider external real-time services or plugins. Bubble's plugin architecture opens possibilities for WebSockets or advanced bridging. But the fact remains that for many typical scenarios—like chat rooms, live dashboards, or transaction tracking—Bubble's built-in approach is usually sufficient.

PERFORMANCE PATTERNS AND LIMITS

Of course, real-time updates can tax your application if you're not careful. Each refresh or triggered update generates server requests. When I designed a live chat feature, I initially polled the database every second. It worked fine with a few testers, but as soon as we had dozens more, performance dipped. The solution was to extend the polling interval slightly and introduce conditions so that the system only fetched fresh messages when something changed in the database.

Properly indexing your data types and optimizing repeating groups also matters. In my projects, using constraints and limiting how much data loads at once was often enough to keep things snappy. Be mindful that more frequent updates require more frequent computing behind the scenes, and your plan's capacity might need to scale. Keeping an eye on logs or Bubble's real-time metrics helps ensure you don't inadvertently hobble responsiveness for the sake of "instant" updates.

THE HUMAN ELEMENT

Adding real-time functionality isn't merely an engineering challenge; it also influences how people interact with your app. The constant flow of data can be exhilarating but sometimes overwhelming. Consider question-and-answer forums, for example. A flurry of new posts might distract from the main conversation. In those cases, I incorporate subtle animations or notifications to let users control when they view updates. Strategically timing those reveals can ensure your interface stays inviting rather than hectic.

Ultimately, real-time updates empower teams to move faster, shoppers to see fresh inventory instantly, and communities to converse fluidly—turning your Bubble project into a dynamic environment that fosters continuous engagement. It's a creative frontier, one where each small feature—like a popped notification or a live data feed—keeps users excited and immersed. As you weave real-time flows into your application, don't be surprised if your audience starts expecting that same immediacy everywhere. Once people taste real-time magic, waiting becomes ancient history.

Chapter 26: Customizing Bubble Templates

THE ALLURE OF A HEAD START

When I started with Bubble, the blank page both thrilled and intimidated me. I was eager to build, but not always certain how to structure a compelling interface or database from scratch. That's when I stumbled upon Bubble's extensive template marketplace. Finding a pre-built design or a near-complete app flow gave me a massive head start. Best of all, I could still bend these templates to my will, infusing my own brand elements and adding unique features.

Yet, I still remember my first near-disaster: I installed a gorgeous landing page template only to discover that I'd inadvertently overwritten chunks of my existing workflows. The experience taught me to treat templates carefully—an amazing resource, so long as you approach them with a robust plan and a willingness to adapt them to your exact vision.

PICKING THE RIGHT FOUNDATION

Today's Bubble marketplace brims with templates covering e-commerce, job boards, social networks, event bookings, and countless more. Choosing a strong foundation involves more than picking whatever looks the slickest. I typically ask: Does the template's core functionality align with my project goals? Is the underlying database structure well-organized? How up-to-date—and how well-rated—is it?

Checking reviews and even running a quick test can pay off. Some templates shine visually but contain haphazard workflows that cause headaches down the line. Others are functionally robust yet dated in design. Striking the right balance between an appealing user interface and a well-thought-out logic layer ensures you're not just inheriting cosmetic flair—you're also adopting a stable architecture.

DISSECTING AND ADAPTING

Whenever I install a new template, I like to dissect it thoroughly before merging it with my main project. That means examining each data type, scanning the workflows, and noting how pages are organized. If something looks messy—like unclear naming conventions or a labyrinth of conditions—I tidy it up first. This step saves me from confusion once I start building advanced features on top of the template.

Then comes the adaptation. Often, I strip away unneeded features, ensuring I keep only elements that support my specific vision. Conversely, if a template is missing a key aspect—like user profiles or a specialized search function—I create placeholders early on. This approach helps me keep the final product cohesive, rather than a patchwork of mismatched elements.

BRANDING AND VISUAL COHESION

A template can provide an excellent layout, but it's still your job to infuse brand identity. I've seen many novices deploy a template's color palette and typography unaltered, resulting in an app that looks eerily similar to others using the same design. That's perfectly fine for quick prototypes, but once you're aiming for a professional release, customizing the style is crucial.

I typically create a brand style guide—colors, fonts, spacing guidelines, even button shapes—and then replace template-based styles systematically. By systematically, I mean opening the Styles tab and swapping out background or text colors across the entire app. The transformation can be astonishing: users see something unique instead of a cut-and-paste product, and your brand resonates consistently across pages.

ENSURING ONGOING COMPATIBILITY

Most templates won't conflict with Bubble's core updates, but keep an eye on major platform changes. If Bubble rolls out a new responsive engine or modifies plugin frameworks, older templates might show quirks. I learned to read developer notes or check user comments about template compatibility. In some cases, you might need to update certain elements or workflows.

One advantage is that many template creators also provide updates or patches. If you rely heavily on a particular template's structure, staying in touch with its developer—whether through email or the Bubble forum—can ease the update process. That said, once you've customized a template extensively, there's often a point of "no return," where automatic updates can break your additions. Balancing convenience with control is key.

EMPOWERMENT THROUGH TEMPLATES

The real power of templates isn't about skipping the creative process; it's about accelerating it. I've leveraged them to jumpstart an MVP in just days, focusing my energy on what made my app distinct. Instead of figuring out how to build a functional signup flow, for instance, I let the template handle it, freeing me to develop a unique matching algorithm or specialized dashboard.

Ultimately, customizing templates is a delicate balance between adopting another developer's blueprint and asserting your own style. When done thoughtfully, it's like inheriting a well-built house that you redecorate and expand upon. You don't demolish the foundation; you adapt it to suit your needs—adding a wing here, reshaping a room there—until it becomes unmistakably yours, shining as a seamless expression of your brand and vision.

Chapter 27: Integrating Payment Gateways

HOW MONETIZATION MEETS YOUR CUSTOMERS

I recall the thrill of my first e-commerce sale: a modest ten-dollar purchase, yet it felt like a million bucks to me. Watching the transaction flow from my Bubble app through a payment gateway signaled that my ideas could generate real revenue. But behind that one click lies a network of processes—authorizations, security checks, confirmations—that can make or break user trust.

Adding payment capabilities to your Bubble project isn't complicated, but it demands careful thought. From selecting a payment gateway to designing a pain-free checkout, every detail must come together smoothly. After all, whether you run a subscription service or sell one-off items, handling money is serious business.

PICKING THE RIGHT GATEWAY

Your gateway choice often hinges on three key factors: where your customers live, what payment methods they prefer, and how much friction you're willing to tolerate. Stripe is commonly favored in the Bubble community—its official plugin simplifies tasks like setting up subscriptions or single payments. PayPal remains a staple too, especially in regions where it's often the default digital wallet.

On occasion, regional payment gateways might offer better local coverage or lower fees. I once built an app for a community in Southeast Asia, opting for a local provider that supported e-wallets popular in that region. The key is ensuring whichever gateway you pick is dependable, transparent about fees, and easy for your audience to use.

IMPLEMENTING SECURE CHECKOUT FLOWS

Bubble's integration steps vary based on the plugin. Typically, you'll install the gateway plugin, configure API keys, and map relevant workflows—such as "When Button is Clicked, create a checkout session." This logic might redirect users to a hosted payment page or embed a checkout form directly within your app.

In my first production app, I used Stripe's hosted checkout, which handled card information securely off my site, reducing my compliance burden. However, if you need a white-labeled approach (where users never leave your domain), you can incorporate gateway elements or use the "Payment Intent" model. Regardless of your path, prioritize data security: let the gateway handle sensitive information while you store only what's necessary, such as a transaction ID.

SUBSCRIPTIONS AND RECURRING BILLING

Recurring payments can transform your income from sporadic transactions to predictable revenue. Stripe's plugin typically allows you to create products and link them to subscription plans. I found it crucial to plan how I'd manage user access or membership tiers once a payment recurred successfully. For example, if someone upgraded mid-cycle, my workflows needed to prorate that subscription or schedule an immediate plan change.

Failing to handle these transitions gracefully can undermine user confidence. We've all encountered messy subscription systems—where you're charged incorrectly or locked out unexpectedly. Bubble's data logic can help you keep everything in sync: store a user's subscription status, next billing date, and any relevant features. Linking these to your privacy rules ensures only paid users gain entry to premium content or advanced functionalities.

AUTOMATIONS AND NOTIFICATIONS

One of the biggest perks of integrated payments is the automation potential. Let's say you want to send a welcome email each time a transaction clears, or issue receipts automatically. With Bubble's workflows and webhooks from your chosen gateway, it's no sweat. Usually, you'll set up an endpoint in Bubble for the gateway to call whenever a payment event occurs—like a successful payment or a subscription cancellation.

From there, you can spool up custom workflows to add credits to a user account, email a summary of what they purchased, or even thank them with a discount code for their next order. Taking advantage of these events can create a polished user experience that prompts repeat business and positive word-of-mouth.

HANDLING REFUNDS AND DISPUTES

Where money flows, disputes eventually follow. Maybe the buyer had a change of heart, or a product wasn't delivered on time. Handling these moments gracefully can make or break your brand's reputation. Gateways like Stripe let you issue partial or full refunds directly through the plugin or via the gateway's dashboard.

One lesson I learned was to plan for refunds in my Bubble workflows. If I rely on a user's payment record for unlocking certain features, I need a contingency if that payment is reversed. For example, the system should automatically revoke access to premium features or revert user credits. By preparing for these scenarios in advance, you empower your users with confident customer support and maintain an honest billing relationship.

Ultimately, integrating payment gateways is about much more than adding a "Pay Now" button. It's about ensuring secure, seamless transactions that earn and maintain user trust. When executed properly, the payment flow feels natural, guiding people from interest to purchase without friction. And once your revenue starts arriving, all those hours spent refining the experience feel well worth it—there's no thrill quite like that first alert from your payment gateway confirming you've made another sale.

Chapter 28: SEO Essentials for Bubble Apps

SOARING ABOVE THE DIGITAL NOISE

Early in my Bubble experience, I focused heavily on design and functionality, assuming that if my product was good enough, people would just find it. Naturally, they didn't. That's when I realized success meant courting the almighty search engines. Search Engine Optimization (SEO) isn't just a trick or a hack—done ethically, it ensures folks searching for solutions can stumble upon yours. With the right approach, Bubble can be just as SEO-friendly as any hand-coded site.

I'm the first to admit that wrangling SEO can feel like tackling an alien language. Keywords, meta tags, structured data—it's a lot. But with Bubble, many of these elements are neatly accessible in your app's Settings and your page-level configurations. Once I discovered them, it was like finding a secret control room for search visibility.

STRUCTURING YOUR PAGES

Google's crawlers and their counterparts love clarity. If your Bubble pages sprawl under a single URL or hide crucial content behind dynamic rendering, it's harder for crawlers to interpret. That's why I started ensuring each core piece of content had its own dedicated page or well-labeled path. For instance, a blog post might be at "/blog/post-title," while a product listing might be

"/products/product-name." This approach helps search engines figure out the hierarchy and context of your site.

Additionally, I carefully used heading tags—**h1** for main titles, **h2** for subtopics—to reflect logical structure. These headings allow both crawlers and visually impaired users (via screen readers) to quickly glean what the content is about.

META TAGS AND PAGE DESCRIPTIONS

In Bubble's "Page SEO" settings, you can specify the title, description, and even social sharing previews for each page. Underestimating these fields is a rookie mistake. A crisp, keyword-rich page title helps search engines categorize your content, whereas the meta description can entice potential visitors to click through.

I once had a landing page with a generic "Welcome to MyApp" meta title. After I changed it to "Streamline Your Tasks I MyApp's Powerful Task Manager," I noticed a bump in traffic—because suddenly, it told searchers exactly what they'd find. I also tested variations of descriptions, seeing which wording best captured user interest. It's a data-driven approach that meets your visitors halfway, matching their keyword intent with your offering.

SPEED AND PERFORMANCE

Search engines heavily weigh performance factors. If your site loads at a snail's pace, it drops down the rankings like a stone. While Bubble manages server optimizations on its end, you can still do your part: compress images, avoid extraneous plugins, and cut down on massive repeating groups. I recall adding a large, high-res background video that looked spectacular. But it also ballooned the page load time, freaking out page-speed analyzers.

Eventually, I replaced it with a lighter image. My bounce rate improved, and so did my search ranking. A second piece of advice is to ensure you use Bubble's lazy loading or pagination features so that only essential content loads first, reducing initial overhead.

MOBILE FRIENDLINESS AND RESPONSIVENESS

More than half of web traffic now comes from mobile devices, so Google ranks responsive sites higher. Bubble's responsive editor should be your ally here. If your content breaks or hides vital data on smaller screens, you'll lose potential visitors before they even start reading. I routinely test each page on small phone screens, medium tablets, and large desktops.

If something looks off, adjusting element alignments or building alternative mobile layouts can salvage your SEO ranking. Google's own "Mobile-Friendly Test" can highlight problem areas, urging you to keep user experience consistent across devices.

QUALITY CONTENT AND URL SHARING

Search algorithms evolve constantly, but one principle endures: quality content outperforms shallow fluff. Bubble's dynamic data fields make it easy to generate fresh pages or content. Let's say you run an events directory—each new event is a chance to rank for terms related to that event's location or topic. As your database grows, so does your footprint in search results.

I also pay attention to social sharing. Crisp Open Graph tags let your page previews look appealing on Facebook, LinkedIn, or Twitter. People are more likely to share if the link preview is enticing—pulling in an image or snippet that teases the value within. And the more your content is shared, the stronger your domain authority becomes over time.

Ultimately, SEO on Bubble boils down to a blend of technical tune-ups and content strategy. It's not about tricking search engines; it's about presenting a polished, valuable experience to both crawlers and humans. The best part? Many SEO optimizations—like improved site speed or structured content—make your app better for every visitor, human or otherwise. It's a win-win approach that transforms your Bubble project from an isolated island into a discovered destination on the vast ocean of the internet.

Chapter 29: Mastering Reusable Elements

TURNING TEDIOUS INTO EFFICIENT

One of my early frustrations in web design was duplicating the same header or footer across multiple pages. If the color needed adjusting or a button label changed, I had to hunt down each instance. It felt like digital whack-a-mole. Then I realized Bubble offered a golden solution: Reusable Elements. By condensing frequently repeated chunks of interface into a single, central design, I could roll out consistent modifications across my entire app with just a few taps.

I vividly recall the relief when I revised a site-wide navigation bar in one fell swoop. No more rummaging through every page to correct a single menu item. Instead, I updated the Reusable Element, and my changes instantly cascaded throughout the app. That moment was pivotal—it showed me how Reusable Elements let you focus on the unique sections of each page, while the familiar blocks handle themselves.

IDENTIFYING REPETITION

First, you need to spot areas that deserve reusability. Typically, these are headers, footers, sidebar menus, pop-ups (like sign-in or cart overviews), or any feature repeated on multiple pages. I once had a site with a small "Contact Us" form that popped up in four different places. Each was identical—except when I wanted to add a phone field. That meant four manual updates. Converting them into a single Reusable Element made the workflow simpler and cut my editing time.

I also look for patterns in user interface modules. For instance, if each user profile has a standard layout (photo, name, short bio, follow button), turning that layout into a Reusable Element ensures uniform design. And if you want to add a new feature—like a "Send Message" button—one edit can apply site-wide.

STRUCTURING YOUR REUSABLE ELEMENTS

To create a Reusable Element, navigate to the Bubble editor's Element Tree and choose "Convert into a reusable element." Alternatively, you can start from scratch by selecting "Add a Reusable Element" from the dropdown. Once it's set, you'll see the element appear in your Reusable Elements folder.

Within that folder, you build the layout, set up events, and define states just like you would on a normal page. The difference? You can now drop this Reusable Element onto any page with a single drag-and-drop. Bubble treats it like a self-contained module, keeping its logic bundled for quick adjustments. You can also pass data into the Reusable Element, letting it display content based on the current user or the page context.

PASSING DATA AND WORKFLOW NUANCES

Handling data inside Reusable Elements can be slightly tricky if you're not aware of how they communicate with the parent page. If I need to display user-specific info, I set the Reusable Element's type of content to "User," for example. Then, whenever I place the element on a page, I can feed it a "Current user" or some other relevant data source.

However, I discovered the importance of carefully managing workflows. If you want the Reusable Element to trigger a page-level workflow (like opening a new pop-up that lives on the parent page), you might set up a custom event or use Bubble's built-in event triggers. Conversely, you can keep everything self-contained inside the element so it's truly modular. My approach depends on whether I need the Reusable Element to remain generic or to interact heavily with page-specific features.

VERSIONING AND MODULAR EVOLUTION

As your project grows, these Reusable Elements evolve too. Maybe your header gains a new dropdown menu, or your user profile card needs a progress bar. In the Bubble development environment, you can safely tweak the element, test it on a dummy page, and only push live once it meets your standards. The instant you deploy, every instance of that element in your app updates in lockstep.

Of course, it's wise to keep backups or versioning for complex Reusable Elements. If you break a crucial bit of logic, you'll want the option to roll back seamlessly. I usually name them clearly—like "Header_nav_v2"—so if something goes awry, I can revert or compare older versions without confusion.

SCALING YOUR EFFICIENCY

Eventually, Reusable Elements become the building blocks of a modular design approach. Instead of churning out pages from scratch, you piece together a puzzle of established reusable pieces: navigation headers, search bars, profile boxes, footers, marketing sections, user dashboards. Each piece is thoroughly tested and brand-consistent. This method not only saves time but promotes a uniform user experience—visitors don't have to relearn how to navigate from page to page because every fundamental component behaves identically.

For me, Reusable Elements have been a design epiphany, bridging the convenience of drag-and-drop with the elegance of modular architecture. They're a testament to how Bubble's no-code philosophy isn't about limiting possibilities, but about nudging you toward systematic, scalable building. Each time I cut hours from my design process—or keep user flows consistent with minimal effort—I'm reminded of how crucial these little building blocks can be. They let you craft a cohesive, professional app that feels like it was assembled with mindful, masterful intention.

Chapter 30: Third-Party Integrations

THE WORLD BEYOND BUBBLE

Not too long ago, I found myself in a situation where my in-house data just wasn't cutting it. Users were clamoring for more functionality—live weather forecasts, currency conversions, and social sharing tools. That's when I realized that the magic of Bubble could extend far beyond its native toolkit. With the right approach, third-party integrations can take an ordinary app and transform it into a multifaceted powerhouse.

PICKING THE RIGHT PARTNERS

The first step in forging these connections is deciding which external services to link. My golden rule is to always ask: "Does this service solve a critical need, or is it just a flashy add-on?" In one project, I connected to a real-estate listing API because accurate property data was essential to user trust. In another, harnessing a time-zone conversion service saved me from manually juggling complex date calculations. By focusing on genuinely useful services, I avoided clutter and kept my interface clean.

MAPPING OUT THE INTEGRATION FLOW

After settling on a service, I always plan out a mini user journey. Let's say I want to display user tweets within my Bubble dashboard. I'll outline each step: authentication, request for specific hashtag data, formatting the returned posts, and then storing them in my local database. Visualizing this flow clarifies how Bubble will communicate in real time with the external API—where the data goes in, how it transforms, and where it lands on the final screen.

LEVERAGING THE API CONNECTOR

One of my favorite Bubble features is the API Connector plugin. It's like the universal translator for RESTful services. All it took me was plugging in the endpoint, setting up parameters, and selecting the authentication needed—maybe an API key or OAuth token. A quick test call usually confirms if everything's wired up correctly.

In a travel project, I used the connector to fetch flight availability. Whenever a user clicked "Search Flights," a workflow triggered the API call, retrieved flight listings, and neatly displayed them in a repeating group. The best part? Everything was done visually. I didn't write a single line of raw code—just toggled some fields, included headers, and let Bubble do the heavy lifting.

HANDLING AUTHENTICATION AND ERRORS

When dealing with user-based data—like pulling someone's social media posts—a secure authentication layer is crucial. I usually rely on services that support token-based authentication, ensuring I don't have to store any sensitive credentials in plain text. Bubble's environment variables or plugin configuration panels simplify this, masking keys to keep them private.

Errors can happen. I learned to handle them gracefully by setting up "on error" workflows, sending friendly messages to users instead of cryptic codes. For instance, if an external weather API times out, my app displays a fallback message: "Unable to fetch the weather. Please try again later." That small courtesy prevents confusion and preserves user loyalty.

DATA TRANSFORMATION AND STORAGE

Third-party data sometimes arrives in a format that's not directly user-friendly. Maybe location data appears as latitude/longitude pairs or product info is wrapped in nested arrays. I deal with this by parsing the JSON or XML responses right in the API Connector. I map each field to Bubble's data types, storing what's relevant in a structured manner.

However, not all data needs to remain in your database. If you're only displaying ephemeral information—like a one-off currency exchange rate—fetching and showing it on the fly might be enough. This approach keeps your database lean while still offering real-time freshness.

EXPANDING APP HORIZONS

Ultimately, incorporating third-party services can catapult your app from "nice" to "indispensable." The possibilities are practically endless: you can integrate mapping services for store locators, CRMs for advanced lead management, or project management boards for collaboration. Each new connection breathes fresh life into your Bubble creation, often spurring even more ambitious ideas.

I'll never forget the thrill of pulling real-time stock quotes into an investment dashboard. Users were amazed to see share prices update at the click of a button. That sense of immediacy gave them confidence in my platform and opened the door to premium features. The moral? Seamlessly blending external data into your workflows creates an app that resonates with real-world needs.

Now, whenever I start a new project, I don't hesitate to consider third-party integrations right from the start. The array of tested, reliable APIs out there means I don't have to reinvent the wheel. Instead, I can focus on user experience and unique selling points while letting these services handle the specialized tasks. That's the real power of the no-code revolution: building robust digital ecosystems without coding them all in-house.

Chapter 31: Security Best Practices

FROM BLISSFUL IGNORANCE TO PROACTIVE SHIELDING

I used to assume that, because I wasn't coding in a traditional sense, my Bubble apps were automatically safe. That was a naïve perspective. One wake-up call arrived when a friend pointed out how my site lacked role-based permissions for administrators—meaning anyone with a direct link might poke around restricted content. Realizing I needed to protect sensitive user data and block potential intruders transformed how I approached development.

ADOPTING A SECURITY MINDSET

Securing an app isn't just about toggling a few settings; it's a mindset. I routinely ask myself what the worst-case scenarios could be. Could someone manipulate the URL to access someone else's data? Could they insert harmful scripts into form fields? By brainstorming these possibilities, I pinpoint my vulnerabilities long before any malicious users do.

LEVERAGING PRIVACY RULES

Bubble's privacy rules are the first line of defense. Through a visually guided interface, I specify who can read or modify each data type. For instance, if I design a user profile, I ensure that only the profile owner or authorized admins can view confidential details like payment info. Similarly, if I'm building a client portal, I can restrict each record so only relevant parties see them.

It took me a bit of experimentation to get comfortable. Early on, I'd accidentally lock out even legitimate users because I over-tightened the rules. Over time, I learned to strike a balance between necessary restrictions and allowing normal usage. Testing these rules from different mock user accounts is essential, so you confirm that the right people see the right data—nothing more, nothing less.

ENFORCING STRONG AUTHENTICATION

Before Bubble, I worried about hashing passwords or handling tokens, but the platform manages much of that under the hood. Still, I can encourage strong user credentials by implementing minimum password requirements or two-factor authentication. While Bubble doesn't natively offer 2FA out of the box, I once integrated a third-party verification service, sending time-sensitive codes to the user's email or phone.

Remember: user sessions should also time out after a certain period. Leaving a session open indefinitely increases the risk someone else could hop onto a device and impersonate the user.

Bubble's settings can automate session timeouts, making your app more foolproof against casual infiltration.

PROTECTING AGAINST COMMON THREATS

Two notorious vulnerabilities still plague online platforms: SQL injection and cross-site scripting (XSS). Although Bubble's no-code environment shields you from raw database queries, user-generated data can still pose a risk. Avoid rendering raw HTML unless absolutely necessary, and consider using text fields or content filters that sanitize inputs.

For any file uploads, I set restrictions on size and type. You don't want users uploading executable files or hidden malware. Bubble's file-handling system can pass these files through scanning services if you connect an external provider—an extra step that's well worth the peace of mind.

KEEPING AN EYE ON LOGS AND ALERTS

I've learned that real-time monitoring can detect shady behavior long before it becomes a crisis. Bubble's built-in logs let me see which workflows are firing, how often, and by whom. If I spot an unusual spike—like hundreds of requests from a single IP address within a minute—I investigate. Maybe it's a genuine surge in traffic, or maybe it's a brute force attack.

Setting up email alerts for specific triggers, such as multiple failed login attempts, keeps me proactive. It's not about living in constant paranoia, but about being ready to intervene quickly if something looks suspicious.

WORKING IN SECURE ENVIRONMENTS

I cherish Bubble's development and live environments for letting me experiment safely, but I also make sure to test my security configurations in a staging or dev environment before going live. That way, I'm confident no security updates inadvertently break user workflows or open loopholes.

Lastly, if you're dealing with sensitive data—like healthcare records—learn the relevant regulations. HIPAA, GDPR, and other laws might demand encryption solutions or specific user consent flows. Bubble offers encryption at rest, but ensure you follow your region's guidelines.

Security isn't a one-time fix. It's an ongoing process of refinement and vigilance. Each new feature could introduce new vulnerabilities, so I check my privacy settings and test user roles again. And though I love the freedom of no-code, I've learned that with great power comes great responsibility: it's up to me to build trust by locking down my app effectively and respectfully. Users who feel safe are far more likely to stick around—and that sense of trust can be a true competitive edge.

Chapter 32: Automated Testing Strategies

WHEN MANUALLY CLICKING ISN'T ENOUGH

For a long time, I tested every new feature by clicking through each page and verifying if it behaved right. This works fine for tiny prototypes, but it starts to crumble once your app grows. Let's say you've got intricate sign-up flows, an interactive dashboard, and multiple user roles. One small tweak to your workflows could break something else without you realizing it. That's where automated testing swoops in like a silent hero— quietly verifying your app's functionality around the clock.

DEFINING YOUR TESTING GOALS

Before diving into any automated testing tools, I found it crucial to define what I wanted to test. Do I care about user interface consistency, or do I need to ensure my data transformations are rock-solid? Some apps require load testing—will 100 people clicking "Buy Now" at once cause a meltdown? Others require rigorous logic checks, like complex calculations. By outlining your top requirements, it's easier to pick or build an automated testing strategy that fits your app's unique traits.

LEVERAGING EXTERNAL TESTING PLATFORMS

Bubble doesn't come with an out-of-the-box automated test runner, but plenty of third-party services fill the gap. Tools like Ghost Inspector or Selenium-based frameworks let you record a series of browser actions. For instance, you might script a test that opens your app, logs in with a credential, navigates to the dashboard, and performs a sample transaction. If any step fails—maybe the login button was accidentally renamed—the test suite will notify you.

Integrating these tools often involves installing a browser extension or configuring a headless browser in the cloud. Once set up, you can schedule test runs daily or each time you deploy a new version. There's nothing quite like the relief of seeing that green "All tests passed" indicator, especially after you've introduced a major feature change.

API-LEVEL CHECKS

In many apps, external or internal APIs handle vital tasks. Whether it's processing user analytics or fetching external data, these endpoints deserve their own checks. I once used Postman's built-in testing to confirm valid responses for each endpoint. For example, if I expect a user endpoint to return "name," "email," and "role," a quick test ensures that a missing field won't slip by unnoticed. You can also gauge performance—spotting slow endpoints before users start complaining about delays.

MAINTAINING A TEST ENVIRONMENT

One of Bubble's biggest advantages is the separation between development and live environments. I extended that idea by creating a dedicated test environment, populated with dummy data that didn't risk messing up real user accounts. Automations could safely run destructive tests—like deleting records or updating fields—without harming production. It also helps to set unique colors or banners in your test environment, so you never confuse it with live.

For especially complex workflows, I often create multiple test scenarios. One might test a new user's sign-up and immediate profile build-out; another tests an existing user upgrading their plan or requesting a refund. This broad coverage reduces the chance of unexpected outcomes once actual people start exploring these features.

CONTINUOUS INTEGRATION AND VERSIONING

If you collaborate with a team, continuous integration (CI) can automate tests whenever someone merges a new branch or feature. While Bubble doesn't have a native CI pipeline, you can still mimic the concept by running your automated browser scripts after each deployment. If the tests detect breakages, you hold off on rolling out changes or revert to an older version. It's a safety net that fosters confidence to experiment more freely in development.

INTERPRETING FAILURES

Automated testing doesn't eliminate errors; it just speeds up your awareness. In fact, you might see more red "failure" indicators when you first adopt testing. At first, I was alarmed—did I suddenly break everything? Actually, my tests were just revealing issues I'd never caught manually. Embracing these failures as valuable signals, rather than inconveniences, aided my ability to fix the root causes swiftly.

A typical real-world example: My sign-up test script failed because I changed the label text from "Create Account" to "Join Us." The button's locator in the script no longer existed. The fix took two minutes, but it reminded me to keep a stable naming convention or to use more robust object identifiers rather than text labels.

KEEPING TESTS UP TO DATE

Automated tests can turn into a mess if left to rot. Each time I revise a workflow or rename a page, I check the relevant test scripts. A quick maintenance pass saves me from sifting through false alarms later. Over time, I build a living library of tests that grows with my application.

Ultimately, automated testing becomes a critical pillar of reliability. It frees me from the monotony of repeated manual checks, letting me tackle bigger features or refine existing designs without fear. Users benefit, too—fewer bugs, smoother updates, and a better overall experience. It's amazing how a few well-structured scripts can transform your confidence level in every new release, reinforcing Bubble's promise of quick iteration with minimal fuss.

Chapter 33: Team Collaboration with Bubble

DISCOVERING STRENGTH IN NUMBERS

I remember the first time I tried to build an app with a friend. We shared endless messages—he'd tweak a workflow, I'd revise a design, sometimes we'd accidentally overwrite each other's work. Although Bubble was built for solo creators at heart, I soon discovered handy features and best practices that made it a fantastic hub for collaborative efforts. When you harness them properly, working together in Bubble can be both painless and productive.

DEFINING ROLES AND ACCESS

When collaborating, the first question is who does what. One person might handle visuals, another might manage the database, and a third might refine workflows. Bubble's editor allows you to add collaborators to the project through a shared team plan or by inviting them individually. However, not all collaborators need full admin privileges. In my experience, giving certain individuals "view only" or limited editing access prevents accidental breakages.

Creating a short guide or "roles document" also keeps everyone on track. For example, I might outline that I handle front-end design, while my co-builder focuses on backend logic. That way, we don't step on each other's toes, rewriting the same elements or tangling each other's workflows.

VERSION CONTROL AND BRANCHING

One of Bubble's underrated features is its versioning system. I treat each version like a branch in traditional software development. If I'm implementing a major new feature, I duplicate the current working version so I can experiment without risking the stable release. Meanwhile, my teammate might remain on the main version, fixing small bugs.

Once I'm satisfied with my changes, I merge them back into the main version. If something catastrophic goes wrong, I revert. This approach fosters a safer environment, reducing those panicked Slack messages like, "Hey, did you just delete our main sign-up page?" The versioning becomes a safety net that encourages bold experimentation—knowing we can always step back to a working snapshot.

COMMUNICATING INSIDE THE EDITOR

While we often used external channels—like Trello or email—to discuss tasks, sometimes we needed quick notes right in Bubble. I began leaving comments on workflows or data types, explaining the rationale behind certain fields or conditions. These comment fields can be literal lifesavers when a new teammate arrives or if we revisit the project months later. Every snippet of context ensures no one scrambles to decode the original logic.

For urgent matters, Bubble's editor might not be enough on its own. In those cases, I keep a dedicated Slack or Discord channel open. The trick is referencing the exact page or element name so people can find it easily. That synergy—fabricating small system of cross-links between the editor and a communication tool—turned out to be a proven recipe for clarity.

DIVIDING AND CONQUERING LARGE FEATURES

Big projects can feel daunting. Maybe your app has multiple modules: an e-commerce store, a chatbot, and a reporting dashboard. Splitting these into separate versions or pages can help each collaborator focus. I once led a team building a fundraising platform. One person managed the donation process, another tackled user profiles, while I handled event ticketing.

We scheduled regular check-ins to see how each module would integrate. Because we standardized naming conventions and design styles, merging felt effortless. By the time we combined everything, it looked cohesive, almost as if a single person had built it (which is precisely what we wanted to convey to end-users).

DE-CONFLICTING CHANGES

Even with perfect planning, conflicts happen. I can't count how many times we both tried to rename the same data field, or I updated a plugin while someone else was testing it. Bubble tries to warn you if two people are editing the same element concurrently. Listening to these prompts saved us from overriding each other's changes. In more significant expansions of the app, we'd timebox ourselves: "You have the next hour to adjust the database, then I'll jump in." It sounds mundane, but scheduling can spare your nerves.

Should a real conflict arise—like changes that accidentally erase crucial logic—Bubble's version rollback often rescues you. I've undone entire sessions just to retrieve a stable state. Then we pick up again, hopefully a bit wiser about coordinating our next move.

FOSTERING A TEAM CULTURE

Collaboration isn't solely about technology; it's about people. Encouraging a culture of transparency—sharing reasons behind each database design, discussing the "why" of a workflow—sparked better synergy. We also did mini "demo days" where we showcased our individual sections. It felt motivating to see each feature come to life and helped everyone spot synergy points or conflicting assumptions early.

In the end, Bubble's capacity for team collaboration changed how I approach projects. Rather than coding diaries in isolation, my colleagues and I co-create dynamic applications in real time. Sure, we've had our share of comedic mix-ups, but each challenge taught us the power of structured collaboration: role definitions, versioning, a communication pipeline, and a dash of patience. When those puzzle pieces fit, Bubble app development transforms into a shared adventure—an adventure that can produce results far more compelling than any solo effort.

Chapter 34: Prototyping for Mobile Devices

A SHIFT IN PERSPECTIVE

I'll never forget the first time I realized that over half of my users were accessing my app via their phones. While I'd tested the desktop layout, the mobile experience looked cramped, with awkward button placements and overlapping text. If you're building in Bubble—or any platform—for the modern world, ignoring mobile design is basically leaving a huge chunk of your audience disappointed. Figuring that out was a turning point in how I prototype new ideas, ensuring they feel at home on smaller screens.

STARTING MOBILE-FIRST

Whenever I begin sketching a new page or feature, I try to visualize how it might appear on a smartphone screen first. In the past, I would design for full-size desktops, then scramble to downsize elements, but flipping that workflow around saves me a lot of headaches. Building a mobile-friendly version from the get-go means my core user experiences never get compromised.

Sometimes, the mobile layout differs drastically. For example, sections that appear side-by-side on desktop might need to stack vertically on mobile. That's not a bad thing—it simply ensures a natural flow for thumb-scrolling. I treat each design choice with a "handheld lens," ignoring the assumption that everyone has a large monitor. That shift in perspective has done wonders for my user retention.

PROTOTYPING TOOLS AND TECHNIQUES

Before investing time in fully designing pages, I often use a wireframing or prototyping tool—like Figma or Balsamiq—to gauge how my layout might scale. I'll draw approximate boxes for a phone's screen size, deciding where the navigation bar sits, how large my images should be, and where forms might appear. Once I'm satisfied with the wireframe, I shift into Bubble's responsive editor to lay out actual elements.

I also keep in mind typical mobile behaviors. For instance, I often place a "hamburger" icon for the main menu, a bottom bar for quick actions, and ensure all tappable buttons meet minimum size guidelines for finger-based navigation—nothing's more frustrating than tapping the wrong link because things are too cramped.

EMBRACING BUBBLE'S RESPONSIVE ENGINE

Bubble's responsive features aren't just about shrinking widths; they're about reorganizing content layers. By setting groups to "collapse margin" or "hide when page width is below X," I can tailor experiences to different breakpoints. For a typical phone layout, I might hide splashy hero images that look terrific on desktop but eat up too much space on a phone. Instead, I greet users with streamlined headings and short calls-to-action.

I also rely on "max width" constraints. If a user with a tablet loads my site, I don't want everything stretched unnaturally. These constraints let me define the sweet spot, ensuring the app remains clean and balanced across a variety of mobile screen sizes.

PERFORMANCE CONSIDERATIONS

Mobile users often have spotty connections compared to Wi-Fi desktops. I learned to keep images compressed and data calls minimal. Pulling a massive dataset on a phone can kill load times or eat someone's data plan. Instead, I rely on pagination or lazy loading. That way, only the top portion of a list appears at first; further rows load as the user scrolls.

Caching also helps speed up returning visits. If you've stored certain assets locally, the app feels zippier on subsequent opens. Combined with prudent data structuring—like not loading entire user histories if I only need the last five entries—I can deliver a near-native feel.

TESTING ON REAL DEVICES

The biggest lesson I learned is that an emulator or a scaled browser window only gets you halfway. Actual devices can reveal surprises—like outsourced font rendering or unexpected scroll bars. I try to test on at least two phones and one tablet. In the best-case scenario, I'll rope in friends who own different Android and iOS models to see if everything lines up.

Once, a friend's older Android phone displayed my images at comically large sizes because of a misread CSS property. If I had relied solely on a Chrome emulator, I'd have missed that quirk entirely. By systematically checking multiple devices, I caught it early, and a quick fix ensured the rest of my users never encountered that glitch.

ITERATING QUICKLY FOR FEEDBACK

When it comes to mobile prototypes, feedback loops matter. Because phone screens can vary so widely, what looks perfect on mine could still fail for someone else. I usually share a preview link with a small group of testers, asking them to record short videos if anything feels off. I pay close attention to input fields and scrolling areas. If they have to pinch-zoom to read text, that's a red flag—time to enlarge those fonts or tweak the layout.

I also keep an ear to user-proposed shortcuts. Maybe they want a floating action button at the bottom right or a simpler way to toggle between pages. Adopting some of these suggestions can significantly improve the user experience, especially when building a product that people might use daily on the go.

Ultimately, prototyping for mobile in Bubble taught me that the phone's constraints are actually creative catalysts. Instead of squishing a full site onto a smaller screen, I focus on the tasks that phone users genuinely need—whether it's a quick check of orders, a swift booking process, or an easy chat interface. By prioritizing clarity, speed, and fingertip-friendly design, I've seen engagement soar. And that's the real payoff: meeting users exactly where they are, phone in hand, ready to explore, interact, and enjoy.

Chapter 35: Transitioning from MVP to Production

FINDING THE RIGHT MOMENT TO SCALE

I've always found the transition from a Minimum Viable Product (MVP) to a fully operational platform to be both exhilarating and nerve-wracking. When I released my first MVP, only a small community of early adopters tested it, helping me note inconsistencies and improvements. But as soon as I sensed a consistent wave of new signups, something clicked: My app was ready for prime time, as long as I could deliver stability, polish, and a strong roadmap.

One of the biggest challenges in deciding the right moment to level up is the tug-of-war between "Is it good enough?" and "Have I tested it enough?" As soon as I realized that my MVP handled core functionality reliably—and that user feedback was more about new features than bug fixes—I took that as a green light to shift gears. Having a clear set of success metrics helped. For me, it was a daily active user count plateauing at a stable number and a consistent record of positive engagement from real customers. Those signals indicated that the MVP had proven its concept, and it was time to become production-grade.

STRENGTHENING ARCHITECTURE AND PERFORMANCE

When moving beyond MVP, I found out the hard way that a haphazard foundation can derail growth. That's when I started diving deeper into Bubble.io's structural features. I re-examined my database setup, making sure my tables and relationships were ready for an influx of new data. I consolidated scattered data types so I wouldn't inadvertently compromise performance with too many complex, redundant relationships.

Additionally, I put advanced caching techniques into place. Bubble itself handles some caching behind the scenes, but I also implemented partial loading for heavy datasets. Rather than serving the entire library to each user, I started serving it incrementally. At scale, every saved millisecond counts. These transformations helped ensure that my newly growing user base experienced smooth browsing, even at peak hours.

BUILDING A SOLID DEPLOYMENT PIPELINE

One of the best decisions I made was formalizing a deployment pipeline, something I had previously brushed aside while working in MVP mode. I created a structured process: develop in a dedicated branch, test intensively in a staging environment, then release it to production after sign-off. Even though Bubble doesn't strictly force me to handle merges like traditional code, the mere act of having a "dev" versus "live" mindset helped me avoid fiascos, such as shipping broken features in a hurry.

That pipeline also introduced more thorough user acceptance testing (UAT). Before any feature reached real customers, a small group of testers attempted to break it. This stage felt like a trial by fire, but it uncovered many potential headaches. Being in MVP mode meant I had initially accepted a level of scrappiness; shifting to production demanded that every major feature pass these more exacting tests.

REFINING UX AND UI CONSISTENCY

In MVP days, I'll admit I allowed some mismatched colors and inconsistent button placements—my priority was validating the concept quickly. But when you go production, even small aesthetic quirks can hurt user perception. That's why I performed a UI audit, systematically reviewing every page for design cohesion. I standardized color palettes, margin spacing, and typography. Whenever I found a leftover MVP design pattern, I replaced it with a polished look.

More than just aesthetics, consistency also keeps user flows intuitive. People should glide from one page to another without feeling lost or having to relearn navigation. By revamping UI elements, I made sure new customers—now discovering the platform—felt that every click was deliberate, every screen was ready for their next step.

PREPARING FOR CUSTOMER SUPPORT AND DOCUMENTATION

One of the biggest mindset shifts from MVP to production is setting up reliable customer support. In the early phase, I could personally reply to each bug report or question, but that was no longer sustainable once my audience began to scale. I added a built-in chat option that linked to a help-desk tool, ensuring users got quick responses and a ticketing system kept track of concerns.

At the same time, I realized that comprehensive documentation is invaluable. I meticulously built a knowledge base for new users. Thorough how-to guides, frequently asked questions, and short video tutorials all saved me hours of repeated explanations later. This was particularly beneficial for enterprise-level clients, who needed confidence in our platform before they'd invest or recommend it internally.

REALIGNING GOALS AND STRATEGY

Finally, transitioning to production means redefining what "success" looks like. In MVP mode, success meant verifying that my idea had a heartbeat—people found it useful enough to return. In production, success meant generating revenue in a sustainable way, fostering ongoing engagement, and continuously iterating based on real user data.

That pivot also forced me to refine my product roadmap. For each new feature request, I evaluated whether it aligned with core objectives or distracted from them. Growing from MVP to production taught me the art of deliberate trade-offs—knowing which improvements add genuine value versus which might bloat the platform.

Once I embraced these changes, I sensed a deeper connection with my user community. They recognized the newfound professionalism, responsiveness, and reliability. That's the priceless payoff: a product that feels truly equipped to shine in the real world. Gone are the MVP disclaimers and disclaimers about "testing in progress." I can now say, with confidence, that my Bubble-powered platform truly stands on its own.

Chapter 36: Creating Admin Dashboards

THE PULSE OF YOUR APPLICATION

I remember the moment I realized I needed a dashboard. My user base was expanding quickly, and I was still hunting through raw data tables whenever I wanted to check stats or resolve issues. It felt like rummaging around in the dark. That's when I envisioned a specialized admin dashboard—a single, centralized control center—to keep tabs on everything from user activity to system health.

Designing an admin interface in Bubble demands a much different approach than building a user-facing page. Here, aesthetics often take a backseat to clarity and efficiency. The tricky part is deciding how much information to reveal. Too little, and you're still forced to do manual checks; too much, and the screen becomes an overwhelming sea of numbers. Striking that balance ensures administrators remain informed without drowning in data.

STRUCTURING KEY METRICS AND WIDGETS

Before building my first admin page, I brainstormed all the metrics I wanted at a glance. User sign-ups per day, transaction volume, open customer tickets—whatever was mission-critical for my situation. Then, I grouped these metrics into widgets on a grid layout. Each widget highlighted a different type of data, often with a line graph or compact table for details.

I discovered that styling each widget with consistent color schemes and consistent sizing helps the dashboard feel cohesive. If new widgets appear in the future—say, a chart for daily active sessions—I can seamlessly drop them in without redesigning the entire page. This modular approach reduces friction down the road.

DRILLING DOWN THROUGH MULTIPLE LEVELS

Sometimes a single stat, such as "120 Orders Today," isn't enough. I wanted the ability to dig deeper, so I created a second-layer view that opened either via click or a plus icon. For instance, clicking on that "Orders Today" widget might expand a list of those orders, letting me see customer names, order totals, and statuses.

These layered dashboards prevented clutter on the main screen while still offering immediate access to deeper context. Essentially, I designed mini secondary pages as pop-ups or side panels. This approach gave peace of mind: If I spot a spike in new sign-ups, I can dig down to see user referral sources or demographic patterns, all without leaving the admin console.

CUSTOM USER MANAGEMENT TOOLS

One feature I quickly learned to appreciate was a simple user management interface. In MVP days, I handled user roles by manually editing database records. That was far from efficient. So, I introduced a dedicated admin panel page listing all users, each row showing role (e.g., basic, premium, admin), status (active or suspended), and the last login date.

From there, I added toggles to suspend individuals or promote them to advanced roles. Doing it visually cut out a lot of guesswork. Plus, if a user triggered any suspicious flags, I'd jump into their detail view—complete with their sign-up IP, current subscription, and usage logs—to investigate issues swiftly.

INCORPORATING NOTIFICATIONS AND ALERTS

A static dashboard can be helpful, but real-time alerts take things to the next level. I established triggers in Bubble that ping my admin dashboard whenever the system encounters certain conditions: a payment error, an atypical user spike, or a sudden flood of support tickets.

To do this, I utilized backend workflows that update a designated field—like "Alerts"—which my admin panel constantly monitors. Whenever a new alert record appears, a bright indicator or pop-up highlights the issue. This proactive element ensures that I'm not always staring at the analytics. Instead, the dashboard summons me when something truly needs immediate attention.

SECURING THE DASHBOARD

Because the admin console grants deep access to user data and system settings, it's vital to keep it safe. I assigned a distinctive user role for administrators, ensuring the dashboard doesn't even render unless you're logged in with that clearance. Bubble's privacy rules help with that, but I took extra steps by restricting the data calls within the admin pages themselves. Even if someone stumbled onto the URL, they couldn't load the sensitive content behind it.

I also integrated IP access filters for an added layer. If I needed to manage the platform from a public Wi-Fi network, I'd pass a two-factor authentication step. That kind of paranoid caution feels warranted once large amounts of information start flowing in.

ITERATING FOR PRACTICAL NEEDS

Officially, an admin dashboard is never finished. Each time you or your team face recurring manual checks, you can convert that friction into a new feature. Maybe you realize you're constantly searching for user feedback from the last 24 hours. That's a sign you should add a dedicated quick filter. Or perhaps your finances team demands a CSV export for accounting. Time to toss in a data export button.

As my business scaled, I kept refining the dashboard, learning from daily usage. What started as a basic stats page grew into a robust system that let me react swiftly to changing circumstances. It's now the unseen engine that ensures everything stays on track, from user satisfaction to revenue targets.

To me, the admin dashboard is the heart of any serious Bubble app, pumping out real-time data and orchestrating crucial tasks behind the scenes. Without it, you're flying blind, guessing at trends and issues. With it, you're empowered to guide your platform, maintain user trust, and steer your project to new horizons, all while confidently clicking through a well-structured interface that you crafted to do exactly what you need.

Chapter 37: Advanced Workflow Tricks

PUSHING BUBBLE'S LOGIC TO THE NEXT LEVEL

I recall the day I realized Bubble workflows could do more than just "Create a new thing" or "Send an email." I was tinkering with a custom event, trying to orchestrate multiple data manipulations in a single user action, when it dawned on me that there's a hidden arsenal of advanced methods waiting to be explored. Over time, I discovered these deeper layers of workflow design can elevate an app from basic forms to a dynamic, near-code-like experience.

The beauty of advanced workflow tricks is that they often reduce manual tasks or complicated logic you'd otherwise handle with custom scripts. Instead, Bubble offers building blocks— conditions, scheduled workflows, and custom triggers—that let you chain complex behaviors without ever touching raw code. It's like discovering bonus levels in a video game you thought you'd already mastered.

ORCHESTRATING MULTI-STEP PROCESSES

One of my first revelations was that a single user action could trigger an entire chain of events. Imagine a purchase button that does more than just record a sale—it updates inventory counts, sends a confirmation email, logs an analytics event, and notifies the shipping department. By carefully sequencing these steps, you ensure all tasks happen in the correct order.

I also embraced the concept of custom events. Instead of repeating the same steps across different workflows, I consolidated commonly used actions into one custom event. For example, "NotifyUserAfterPurchase" stored my standard post-purchase tasks. Any time a user completed a transaction— whether a direct buy or a subscription sign-up—I'd invoke "NotifyUserAfterPurchase," confident that it handled all those routine follow-ups. This modularity saved me from duplicating logic.

USING CONDITIONAL WORKFLOW BRANCHES

I came to appreciate Bubble's conditional branching once I built an app that served multiple user types. Let's say you have a teacher user and a student user. When they both click the same "Submit Homework" button, you might want different behind-the-scenes actions to fire. By layering "Only when Current User's Role = Teacher" or "Only when Current User's Role = Student," I effectively built branching paths within the same workflow.

This approach streamlines your logic. Instead of having separate workflows for each user role, you unify them, ensuring minimal duplication. It also keeps debugging simpler: if something goes awry, you know exactly which condition to examine.

AUTOMATING COMPLEX CALCULATIONS

Sometimes, I need to run multi-step calculations—like scoring a quiz or generating a quote for a custom product. In a naive approach, you might do each step on a separate user action, forcing them to click "Next" repeatedly. But advanced workflows let you chain these calculations seamlessly.

I built a real-time quote generator for a client. When the user clicked "Get Estimate," the workflow tallied item costs, threw in a dynamic discount if the user was a premium member, converted the total to the user's preferred currency, then displayed the final figure. The entire process ran in a heartbeat. This integrated approach doesn't just dazzle your audience—it also sets the stage for a frictionless user experience.

PARALLELIZING TASKS WITH BACKEND WORKFLOWS

I used to worry that tying multiple big tasks to a single user click could slow down the interface. That's when I discovered the power of scheduling backend workflows. Once triggered, they run independently, allowing the user to move on instead of waiting for everything to finish.

For instance, a large data migration or file processing step might run in the background after an admin initiates it. The admin receives a notification when it's done, rather than being stuck on a loading screen. Not only does this keep the front-end snappy, it also prevents timeouts or partial data updates.

BUILDING COMPLEX CONDITIONALS

I still remember the first time I stacked multiple conditionals on a single element. By layering "and" and "or" statements, I could create nuanced logic—like showing a message only if a user was both a premium member and had completed a certain prerequisite. This kind of granularity truly sets Bubble apart from simpler drag-and-drop builders.

Eventually, I realized these conditionals could also handle real-time adjustments to page elements. For example, if a user updated their shipping location, the available shipping methods would auto-adjust, and relevant discounts would appear instantly. It felt like a small miracle of reactivity that replaced a lengthy chain of separate workflows.

DEBUGGING AND TRACKING WORKFLOW PERFORMANCE

With more intricate workflows comes the need for better debugging. Bubble's debug mode lets me step through each action, verifying that the right conditions pass, the correct variables update, and no errors sneak by. When something unexpected occurs, I comb through logs or temporarily embed "Alert" actions that reveal the current state of variables mid-workflow. This hands-on approach acts like a detective's lens, guiding me to the offending step.

Performance matters, too. Scheduling too many concurrent workflows can bog things down. Keeping an eye on capacity usage, and distributing intensive tasks among multiple scheduled events, ensures a stable experience for both you and your users.

These advanced workflow tricks might take a bit of trial and error to master, but once you do, they'll feel like second nature. Every new feature or challenge that arises sparks a thought: "How can I orchestrate this with my existing logic?" Over time, you'll craft a tapestry of orchestrated workflows that handle everything from real-time notifications to big data transformations in the background. And the best part? You'll pull it off without writing a single line of code, yet all the complexity remains elegantly under your control.

Chapter 38: Building Multi-User Platforms

GOING BEYOND SOLO EXPERIENCES

When I first dipped my toes into web app design, my default assumption was that each user would interact with my creation independently—like a personal to-do list or a single-player game. Then one day, I imagined a scenario where multiple users needed to collaborate or share data. That simple shift in mindset led me down the path of building multi-user platforms, where communities and teams could thrive together under one digital roof.

Bubble doesn't inherently limit you to single-user flows, but planning for multi-user functionality requires foresight. The typical "User" data type remains crucial, but you also start exploring new ways to link those user records to shared objects, permission rules, and communal data sets. Once you wrap your head around that, you realize your app can become a meeting place, a marketplace, or even a virtual office space.

DEFINING ROLES AND PERMISSIONS

When multiple people interact with a system, not everyone should have the same rights. If you're launching a project management tool, you might have "Project Owners," "Collaborators," and "Viewers." Each role sees and does different things. In Bubble, I map roles into the user data type as text fields or option sets. Then, using privacy rules, I restrict certain data or pages to relevant roles.

On top of that, I've found it valuable to implement role-specific user interfaces. Suppose an "Admin" logs in—maybe they see a dashboard with the ability to approve or remove content, whereas a "Member" sees only their personal area. This approach avoids accidental tampering. It's all about layering clarity: who can create, who can edit, and who can view only.

COLLABORATION FEATURES AND REAL-TIME SHARING

Some multi-user platforms revolve around shared content, like a group document or a shared spreadsheet. Although Bubble doesn't offer a native real-time collaborative text editor—like Google Docs—you can approximate a simultaneous editing experience through frequent auto refresh or scheduled workflows. Each user sees updates within seconds, forging that sense of collaborative synergy even if it isn't perfectly synchronous.

One simpler method is enabling a "commenting system." Let's say I built a design review platform. Each design entry holds a list of comment records. As soon as someone posts feedback, a refresh or an event-based workflow updates everyone's view. This fosters a communal atmosphere: no one works in isolation, they post, respond, revise, and keep the creative energy flowing.

USER PROFILES AND SOCIAL ELEMENTS

Sometimes, multi-user experiences are social by nature—like a social network or a membership community. Then it's crucial to let each user express themselves. I incorporate profile pages where each user can upload an avatar, personal description, or relevant preferences. If I aim for deeper engagement, I add "Follow" or "Friend" features, enabling people to track each other's updates.

To keep privacy manageable, I build toggles: "Public," "Friends Only," or "Private." This allows users to set their comfort level. The key is ensuring intuitive controls, so people easily grasp what information is visible to strangers versus to the community at large. Thanks to Bubble's conditional logic, toggling these preferences can instantly hide or reveal data in the user interface.

GROUPS, TEAMS, AND WORKSPACES

Whenever an app brings together multiple people under a common goal—like a sports club organizing events or a professional team tracking projects—I create a "Group" or "Team" data type. Each group points to a list of users. By referencing the group in tasks, documents, or posts, the system instantly knows who belongs and what they can see.

Say I'm building a tutoring platform. Each class could be a "Group" data type with a "class name," "instructor," and a list of "students." Shared resources, like reading assignments, automatically become visible to that group alone. This method helps me scale: as new classes form, they each get a new group record, neatly partitioning content and membership.

NOTIFICATIONS AND ACTIVITY FEEDS

Multi-user platforms shine when people stay in the loop about relevant events. That's why I often integrate notifications. If user A comments on user B's post, user B gets an alert. If a manager updates a project's deadline, the team sees a new item in their feed. In Bubble, you can build these notifications by creating a "Notification" data type, tying it to the relevant user, and then displaying the new messages in real time.

To make it more dynamic, I might define categories—"comment," "mention," or "system update"—each with a unique icon or text style. This ensures that as your platform grows, you can keep notifications organized, enabling users to quickly see what matters to them instead of drowning in an indiscriminate list.

PREVENTING OVERLAPS AND MAINTAINING DATA INTEGRITY

One hidden pitfall of multi-user environments is concurrency. If two people attempt to update the same record at once, you can get collisions. Bubble handles some concurrency behind the scenes, but to be safe, I set up "last updated" timestamps. If the record changed in the last few seconds, I require the user to refresh before pushing a second edit. This small step helps avoid overwriting each other's data.

I also rely on validation checks—like ensuring that only group owners can remove members, or that a user can't join more than a certain number of teams. These constraints keep your platform logical and protect it from accidental data sprawl.

Ultimately, building multi-user platforms in Bubble expands your realm of possibilities. You stop crafting apps for solitary consumption and start enabling communities, collaborations, or businesses to flourish collectively. The synergy unfolds as soon as you see multiple people logging in, dividing tasks, or chatting about shared goals. And each small success paves the way for bigger ambitions—the platform can morph into a living, breathing ecosystem that benefits everyone involved.

Chapter 39: Internationalization and Localization

STEPPING ONTO A GLOBAL STAGE

The day I got an email from someone in France who wanted to use my app in their language was the day I realized how important internationalization (i18n) can be. At first, I figured all I needed was a neat way to swap out text strings—but as I dug deeper, I discovered that creating a truly localized experience is more than just translation. It includes adapting formats for numbers, dates, and even color or imagery preferences. Bubble doesn't impose a single method to handle i18n, but it provides enough flexibility to make your app feel right at home in multiple regions.

PLANNING FOR MULTIPLE LANGUAGES

When I first set out to support a second language, I identified all the textual content scattered across my pages—headings, button labels, error messages. I quickly realized that rummaging through each element would be painful if I wanted to add a third or fourth language down the line. That's when I crafted a localization framework. I used a new data type called "Language Strings," storing key-value pairs (like a dictionary): the key was "BTN_LOGIN," while the value was "Log In" in English, "Connexion" in French, and "Iniciar Sesión" in Spanish.

This approach meant I could easily fetch the correct label using a fast query: "Search for Language Strings where Key = BTN_LOGIN and Language = X." By doing so, standardizing new translations felt less random. Whenever I added a new page, I'd define the textual elements in my dictionary. Sure, it took some upfront work, but it paid off when I added additional languages without rewriting each screen from scratch.

DETECTING USER LOCALE AND PREFERENCES

After building my translation dictionary, I needed a way to figure out which language to display. Some apps ask the user to pick a language on their first visit, while others detect browser locale automatically. Bubble can read the user's browser language, so you can set a default. You might store this choice in the user's profile for future logins, effectively letting them switch languages in settings if they want.

For me, letting the user choose felt more natural. People often use devices set to one language but prefer another for certain apps. I integrated a small dropdown in the header for "English / Français / Español," instantly reloading the relevant text from the dictionary. My testers lived in different countries, and they liked having immediate control, no system-level fiddling required.

FORMATTING DATES, TIMES, AND NUMBERS

A common oversight is focusing purely on text while ignoring numeric or date-time formats. I learned quickly that mm/dd/yyyy might confuse users accustomed to dd/mm/yyyy. Similarly, decimal separators switch between commas and periods in various regions. Bubble helps with some date formatting, though you often have to handle custom logic for numeric fields.

Let's say you store an amount as a standard numeric type. For each display event, you can apply a format rule based on the user's chosen locale. If they're set to French, you might show "1 000,50 EUR" instead of "$1,000.50." Even small details, like currency symbols' positions, can improve that sense of belonging for international users.

HANDLING RIGHT-TO-LEFT LAYOUTS

Once you start supporting languages like Arabic or Hebrew, you face multiple alignment challenges. A layout that's left-to-right for English or Spanish needs flipping for right-to-left. Bubble's responsive engine doesn't automatically invert the entire interface, so some manual adjustments are necessary.

What I did was create a separate stylesheet for right-to-left languages. When the user's language property matched "ar" or "he," the body's direction property switched to "rtl," and the container elements flipped. I also verified each page to ensure repeating groups and text elements looked coherent. It may take extra effort, but delivering an app that feels truly native to right-to-left speakers can open huge opportunities in those markets.

PREPARING VISUALS AND CULTURAL NUANCES

Text and data formats aside, localization sometimes demands aesthetic changes. Certain images might convey different messages in different regions. Colors, gestures, or icons may carry unique cultural significance. For instance, a thumbs-up icon is not universally positive, so I replaced it with a more neutral "checkmark" in some versions of my app.

Even time scheduling can differ—some countries have a weekend on Friday and Saturday. If your platform organizes events, acknowledging those variations fosters trust. The deeper you dive, the more you see localization is about empathy. You're inviting a global audience to feel at ease, rather than shoehorning them into a single worldview.

TESTING WITH NATIVE SPEAKERS

Words or phrases that feel right in direct translation might sound off to a native speaker. "Log In" can translate differently based on context. That's why I learned to recruit native testers or use professional freelance translators. They'd catch things like awkward wording or incorrectly conjugated verbs.

I also built quick toggles: "Show me the dictionary entries" to verify every label was accounted for. This helped me systematically confirm that no leftover English strings sneaked into the French UI. Hilariosly, I once had a user mention a random "Submit" button in the middle of an otherwise fully translated page—that line was lodged in a condition I hadn't updated.

MAINTAINING FLEXIBILITY OVER TIME

Localization is never truly "finished." You keep adding new features, new text, or fresh pages, requiring more dictionary entries or revised formats. That's why I rely on a consistent naming scheme for each key. If a new feature arrives, I mark its textual elements carefully. Over time, my dictionary becomes a living resource that must be updated in tandem with development.

The reward? Watching your user base expand into territories you never imagined. Nothing compares to that rush of seeing a user in

Japan or Brazil navigate your site with ease. It feels like transforming a local project into a worldwide phenomenon—one that speaks to every visitor in their native tongue, reflecting genuine respect and welcoming them wholeheartedly into the community you've built.

Chapter 40: Future Innovations in No-Code Development

Over the past few years, I've watched the no-code philosophy evolve from a novel concept into an industry-shaping movement. Initially, many saw "no-code" as a stopgap for those who couldn't program—something neat for prototyping but not truly "serious" development. Fast-forward to our present reality, and we see entire tech ecosystems built on visual design tools, thousands of no-code products powering thriving businesses, and a new wave of creators who approach software building with fresh, unencumbered perspectives. Instead of being a mere substitute for traditional development, no-code has morphed into a transformative way to bring ideas to life.

EMERGING AI-ASSISTED CREATION

When I think about the future, one of the first trends that fires my imagination is the integration of artificial intelligence into no-code platforms. Picture AI-driven assistants that generate app layouts, workflows, and data structures based on casual user inputs. Instead of carefully dragging and dropping elements onto a page, we'll be describing our visions in natural language, and AI will propose ready-made solutions. Early adopters are already experiencing glimpses of it—for instance, auto-generating database models or receiving AI suggestions for streamlined workflows. But, as I see it, this is only the beginning.

Such AI-driven wizards could learn from patterns across thousands of apps and instantly apply these best practices to each new project. Imagine a prompt like, "Build me an app to schedule online appointments," and the AI conjures up not only the user interface but also the behind-the-scenes logic for handling notifications and cancellations. Over time, these systems might refine themselves by watching real users interact with the generated apps, recognizing friction points and autonomously patching them before a human developer even notices a snag.

GREATER INTEROPERABILITY WITH TRADITIONAL CODE

Another leap forward will be bridging no-code with pro-code in truly harmonious ways. Right now, the general model is a clean divide: You either build entirely within a visual environment, or you revert to custom code for advanced manipulations. But I can foresee a world where no-code platforms treat third-party code snippets as modular blocks—almost like "plugins on steroids." Rather than placing code behind black-box APIs, you might visually orchestrate code blocks inside your workflows, letting the best of both worlds collide.

This could spark fresh collaboration between code-savvy developers and no-code enthusiasts. Imagine handing off a specialized piece of functionality—a payment calculation or an AI model—and letting the rest of the team integrate and tweak it visually. That interplay would reduce friction and encourage broader skill-sharing. Consequently, apps would grow more robust without losing the agility that no-code fosters.

ADVANCED DATA VISUALIZATION AND ANALYSIS

No-code tools excel at building functional websites and apps quickly, but data analysis and visualization often still require third-party solutions. Looking ahead, I see platforms doubling down on built-in analytics modules for everything from real-time usage stats to sophisticated business intelligence dashboards. These modules will allow creators to slice, dice, and present data with zero custom code, enabling even non-technical stakeholders to interpret patterns at a glance.

We might see bubble-style chart editors that let you design multi-layered visuals, or auto-updating boards that highlight anomalies and trends using machine learning. I'm anticipating a day when no-code platforms can tap into large data lakes, retrieve subsets of information, apply transformations, and display interactive graphs—all with minimal user effort. This shift will supercharge decision-making cycles, democratizing insights that once required specialized data teams.

NO-CODE FOR HARDWARE AND IOT

An exciting frontier for no-code is bridging physical products—like sensors, wearables, or microcontrollers—with easy-to-design software interfaces. Traditionally, the Internet of Things (IoT) has been the domain of hardware engineers wrestling with firmware and arcane communication protocols. But if no-code platforms step in, connecting devices through drag-and-drop logic, everyday makers could prototype solutions like climate monitoring or smart-home automations without writing firmware from scratch.

We're already seeing glimpses of IoT frameworks that let you visually define rules—like "If sensor X detects temperature above 80°F, send an alert to user's phone." In the not-too-distant future, I believe these ecosystems will expand: hooking up multiple devices, forming networks of sensors, and orchestrating them all from a single no-code dashboard. This evolution will lower the entry barrier for tinkering with hardware, spawning a fresh wave of creativity in fields like environmental science, home automation, and wearable tech.

EXPANDING COLLABORATIVE FEATURES

Lastly, I see collaboration taking on a bigger role in no-code's trajectory. Right now, we can share projects or invite others as co-editors. But imagine real-time, multi-user editing with sophisticated versioning, integrated chat, and even project management boards built directly into the platform. This environment would mimic the collaborative flow of shared documents—no more scheduling separate calls to finalize a design. Everyone would manipulate the same canvas simultaneously, discussing changes in context.

We could also see no-code platforms blossoming into global marketplaces, connecting creators of templates, plugins, and specialized building blocks. This would resemble an app store for entire micro-features. With a few clicks, you'd add a "gamified leaderboard" or "contextual chatbot" to your app, each built and maintained by domain experts. As a result, the speed of iteration would skyrocket, propelling no-code from a productivity booster to a massive network of shared innovation.

The future of no-code, in my view, is dazzling and wide open. It's a realm where boundaries blur—between developer and user, code and drag-and-drop, local and global. As AI, data analytics, and collaboration merge with visual creation, the potential to bring even the wildest ideas to life multiplies. Ultimately, we stand on the edge of a new paradigm, one in which everyone has the power to shape the digital world rather than merely consume it. And if that isn't inspiring, I don't know what is.

www.ingramcontent.com/pod-product-compliance
Lightning Source LLC
LaVergne TN
LVHW052100060326
832903LV00060B/2451